Speed QUILTING

Projects Using Rotary Cutting & Other Shortcuts

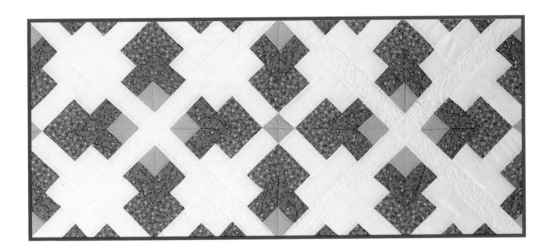

CHERYL FALL

STERLING PUBLISHING CO., INC. NEW YORK

This book is dedicated to my husband Tony, and daughters, Rebecca and Ashley—my sources of inspiration! Your help and patience has been wonderful. With a family like this, I should be able to write a few thousand books before old age hits.

I would like to extend a heartfelt thank you to the following companies for their help in making this book a reality by providing supplies for the models in the book: VIP Fabrics, Concord House Fabrics, Coats & Clark, Freudenberg Nonwovens/Pellon, Fairfield Processing, and JHB International. And a special thank you to a terrific editor, Isabel Stein. She's creative, patient, and always willing to lend a supportive comment.

Text photographs by Jay Turner, Vancouver, Washington
Front cover photograph by Nancy Palubniak, New York City

We have made every effort to ensure the accuracy and completeness of the patterns and instructions in this book. However, we cannot be responsible for human error, or for results when using materials other than those specified in the instructions, or for variations in an individual's work. Neither the author nor Sterling Publishing assumes any responsibility for any damages or losses incurred that result from the use of this book.

Library of Congress Cataloging-in-Publication Data

Fall, Cheryl.
   Speed quilting : projects using rotary cutting & other shortcuts /
by Cheryl C. Fall.
      p.   cm.
   Includes index.
   ISBN 0-8069-1328-2
   1. Quilting—Patterns.   2. Rotary cutting.   I. Title.
TT835.F3375   1996
746.46—dc20   95-22914
                                                                CIP

10   9   8   7   6   5   4   3   2   1

Published by Sterling Publishing Company, Inc.
387 Park Avenue South, New York, N.Y. 10016
© 1996 by Cheryl Fall
Distributed in Canada by Sterling Publishing
% Canadian Manda Group, One Atlantic Avenue, Suite 105
Toronto, Ontario, Canada M6K 3E7
Distributed in Great Britain and Europe by Cassell PLC
Wellington House, 125 Strand, London WC2R 0BB, England
Distributed in Australia by Capricorn Link (Australia) Pty Ltd.
P.O. Box 6651, Baulkham Hills, Business Centre, NSW 2153, Australia
Printed and bound in Hong Kong
All rights reserved

Sterling ISBN 0-8069-1328-2

Contents

CONTENTS

PROJECTS

Preface

In these days of tight schedules and busy lives, making something with your own hands may seem impossible. Children, work, and other commitments can make spare time for sewing and quilting sparse. That's why I wrote this book. *Speed Quilting* is designed for the person who loves to sew, but whose time is limited. The projects in this book use simple, quick-to-stitch techniques and even if you only have an hour or so to spare at a time, you can make something lovely for your home or for a friend in a minimal amount of time. In fact, most of these projects only take 2 to 8 hours to complete. You can make a quilt in a day or a weekend, or work a little each time you have a moment over a few days. It's fun to finish a project quickly, because you can then go on to the next one! You can make many projects and try out all those fun fabrics you've been collecting. The projects in this book were designed for rotary cutting and machine appliqué and quilting.* The projects in this book make lovely gifts that you can create in no time—or make them for your own home to add a splash of color to the corner of any room. With the easy-to-follow directions, it's no problem to pick up where you left off if you need to put your project aside for a while.

Happy quilting,

Cheryl

---

*However, you don't *have* to use machine appliqué or rotary cutting. The instructions also include information for people who prefer to do hand appliqué and cut with a scissors.

Basic Techniques

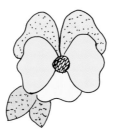

Rotary Cutting

The beauty of rotary cutting is in the fast *precise* results you get. Cutting with the rotary cutter is much more accurate than cutting with scissors. Because you can cut several thicknesses of fabric at once, rotary cutting is very, very fast. To prepare your fabric for rotary cutting, prewash and dry it, and fold it in half with the selvedges together and iron it. Try to iron it so that the fold is directly along the grain of the fabric (the warp or lengthwise grain, in this case). The whole width (selvedge to selvedge) of your fabric should fit on the rotary cutting mat, so fold it again in quarters on the lengthwise grain if it doesn't. Then line up the top fabric fold on a horizontal line of your rotary cut-

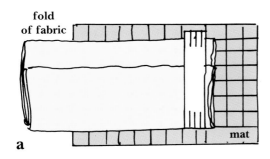

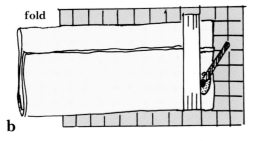

1: Rotary cutting. **a:** *Evening up the jagged raw edge.* **b:** *Cutting strips.*

ting mat. The raw edges probably aren't perpendicular to the top fold (they aren't squared up), so use your see-through plastic ruler and line it up with the first vertical line on the mat that is a bit in from the raw edge of the fabric. Put the ruler's short edge on the fold of the fabric (see figure 1a). Hold the ruler with your left hand, and put your rotary cutter against the ruler with the blade side closest to the ruler at the fold of the fabric closest to you. Press down firmly on the cutter until you feel it go through all the layers of fabric and reach the board. Then push the cutter away from you, keeping it against the ruler, and trim off the uneven edge of the fabric, without stopping until you reach the far end or fold of the fabric. To cut a strip, you simply measure off the necessary width of the strip on your mat and move your ruler in from the trimmed raw edge of the fabric the necessary strip width (see figure 1b), and cut the same way as you did for evening up the edge. You'll learn to recognize the sound of the cutter when it cuts through all the layers of fabric, which will tell you when you have cut through. Remember to always cut away from you when using a rotary cutter. If you notice that your blade starts to skip or miss threads on the fabric you are cutting, it's time for a new blade. Don't use a rotary cutting blade on paper—it will dull the blade in a hurry. Instead, use an old rotary blade for cutting paper, remembering to change back to the other blade when cutting fabric. See the tools section for more details on rotary cutters, mats, and rulers.

Machine Piecing

After cutting all of the necessary pieces, machine stitch the pieces together with their right sides facing and a ¼″ seam allowance (see Fig. 2). Always use a neutral-colored thread to piece your quilt; however, if

2: Machine piecing; stitching two pieces together.

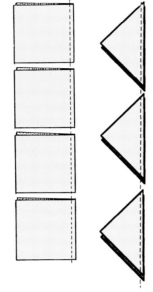

3: Chain piecing multiple units to save time.

there is too much contrast in the fabrics to use a neutral thread, choose a thread that is one shade darker than the *lightest* fabric in the project.

All of the construction in this book is done with ¼″ seam allowances, which are included in all of the pieces you are told to cut. (The appliqué patterns are given without seam allowances, which aren't needed in machine appliqué with satin stitch, however.) If you are unsure of stitching an exact ¼″ seam allowance when machine piecing, measure ¼″ from the right side of the needle and place a small piece of masking tape so its right edge falls at the ¼″ mark on your sewing machine. Use this tape as your stitching guide.

To save time, chain piece when possible. Align all the pairs of pieces to be joined with their right sides facing, and feed them through the machine one pair at a time, butting but not overlapping the units. Continue to stitch the units without cutting the thread between the units (figure 3). When you have sewn all of the units, clip the connecting stitches between the units to separate them.

A Note on Borders

The quilts in this book all require ¼″ seam allowances. However, unless you're an absolutely, positively perfect stitcher, your work will no doubt vary from this rule. Normally, the seam allowances taken are a bit larger than ¼″. If you've cut your border strips to size, but due to variations in your work the strips are too long, here's a hint for trimming the strips.

For the side borders, measure down the center of the quilt and cut the strips to this measurement. Do not measure the sides of the quilt, as they may each be a different length, and you need a common measurement. To stitch the borders in place and consequently square-up the quilt, stitch the borders so that the longer length of fabric is against the feed dogs, be it the border strip or the quilt. For example, if the left side of the quilt top is a bit longer than the strip, place the quilt top face up against the feed dogs and the border strip on top, wrong-side up. The action of the feed dogs will help ease the extra fabric on the quilt top to fit the border strip. If the border strip is longer than the side of the quilt top, place the border strip face up against the feed dogs and the quilt top on top, wrong-side up. Repeat the same steps if necessary for the upper and lower borders.

Remember to use a patchwork or piecing foot when you can. These feet are available for just about all machines and have a perfect ¼″ side on the foot, for accurate piecing. They rarely are included in the machine's supplies, so check with your local sewing machine dealer to purchase one for your model. If you do not wish to use this type of foot, you can mark a guide for the ¼″ seam allowance on the machine bed by placing a piece of masking tape so its edge is exactly ¼″ from the needle. However, I do recommend the feet over this method.

Pressing to Perfection

Get into the habit of *always* pressing your seam allowances after stitching. (Remember: stitch and press, stitch and press—got it?) To press properly, press along the seam line *before* opening out the joined pieces. This will set the seam. Open out the pieces so that the seam allowance is pressed towards the darker fabric and press again, setting the seam allowance into position (figure 4a).

To save time, try to set aside groups of units to be pressed—this way you won't feel as if you're constantly bouncing from the machine to the ironing board! Also, don't use an iron with an automatic shutoff feature if you plan on sewing for any length of time— you'll be constantly re-starting the thing!

When pressing pieces with intersecting seam lines, press each set of seam allowances in opposite directions (figure 4b). This reduces the bulk you will be quilting through later.

Always be sure to press with a *dry* iron. Steam can stretch and distort the pieces, and you need to keep them as accurate as possible for proper piecing.

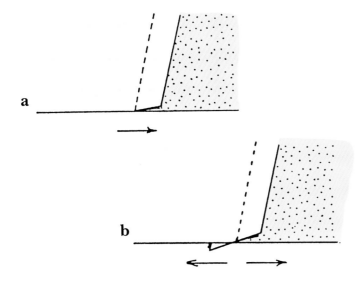

4: *Pressing seam allowances.* **a:** *Press single seam allowance towards the darker fabric.* **b:** *Press intersecting seam allowances in opposite directions.*

Appliqué Basics

The word *appliqué* comes from a French word that means "put on" or "applied." In appliqué, a cutout decoration of fabric is laid on and sewn to a larger piece of fabric. Appliqués may be sewn on by machine or by hand.

Machine appliqué

Machine appliqué is faster, so it's your most likely choice for speed quilting. The attaching stitches are more visible than hand appliqué stitches, and it is both fun and easy to do once you know the proper method of stitching. If you've had problems in the past, try it again using the following tips—you won't be disappointed!

After cutting the base fabric on which your appliqués will be sewn, lightly trace the entire block design onto the base fabric with a water-soluble pencil or other nonpermanent marking tool. This will help you with the placement of the appliqués when you secure them to the base fabric.

The machine appliqué instructions in this book suggest you use fusible transfer webbing to secure the appliqués before they are stitched to the base fabric with satin stitch. Fusible webbing comes in many kinds and weights, but what you need for appliqué work is lightweight and is coated on both sides with a heat-sensitive material that fuses to the fabric when you press it with a warm iron. (Follow the individual manufacturer's instructions about how hot to make the iron, etc.)

In general, press rather than moving the iron back and forth, which may pull up the appliqué. Try to get fusible webbing with paper on one side, which makes it easy to trace your appliqués directly onto the paper side. Choose lightweight fusible webbing so it isn't too difficult to stitch through. Trace the *reversed* appliqué shapes onto the paper side of the fusible webbing. (The appliqué will be facing in the *opposite* direction after it has been fused and cut out, which is why it's necessary to reverse any patterns that aren't symmetrical before you trace them onto the webbing.) Cut out the appliqué shape roughly from the webbing. Fuse the webbing appliqué shape to the *wrong* side of the fabric from which you want to make the appliqué (figure 5a). Then carefully cut the appliqué out of the fabric, following your traced lines of the appliqué shape (figure 5b). No seam allowance is necessary for machine appliqué with satin stitch. Remove the paper backing and fuse your appliqué in place on your base fabric.

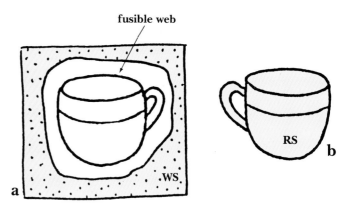

5: *Using fusible webbing for appliqués.* **a:** *The reversed appliqué piece, traced onto fusible webbing and fused to the wrong side of the appliqué fabric.* **b:** *The cut-out appliqué, right side up.*

To sew the appliqué in place, position a piece of tear-away stabilizer that is slightly larger than the appliqué design against the *wrong* side of the base fabric (figure 6). The stabilizer will keep your machine from shoving the fabric through the hole in the sewing machine's throat plate as you stitch, and it will keep your stitches from puckering, which is the reason stabilizer is very important. Stabilizer is available in fabric stores; tracing paper may also be used.

Set the sewing machine to a medium-width satin stitch, and thread the machine with thread that matches the color of the appliqué. Use a neutral thread in the bobbin.

Before you start your actual project, stitch a sample appliqué on scrap fabric and examine it. Does the bobbin thread pull to the top? If so, you have incorrect tension on your machine. Loosening the upper

6: The stabilizer is cut slightly larger than the base fabric and is pinned to the wrong side of the fabric.

tension slightly should correct the problem. If it doesn't, replace your needle. A dull needle or one with burrs can cause your machine to stitch incorrectly. Use a size 9 or 11 universal point needle. Make any other necessary adjustments, such as stitch width or length, before you start your actual project.

Satin stitch

The most popular machine appliqué stitch is the satin stitch. Because satin stitches are very close together, they cover the raw edge of the appliqué. In the satin stitch, the left swing of your needle should be in the appliqué itself, and the right swing should be in the base fabric (figure 7).

To machine appliqué at right-angled corners, stop the needle at the outer point of the appliqué. Raise the presser foot and swing the base fabric around so the next edge is in position and continue stitching

(figure 7c). If the appliqué piece comes to a narrow point, taper the width of your satin stitch as you stitch along the point (figure 7a). You can gradually increase it again on the other side of the point.

To machine stitch a curved or circular piece, you will need to stop stitching and pivot the fabric frequently to get a nice smooth curve. To do this on an outside curve, stop the needle in the base fabric and turn the work slightly (figure 7b). Repeat until you have finished stitching the entire curve. To stitch an inside curve, pivot the work in the same manner, but stop the needle in the appliqué piece instead.

Other machine stitches

Other stitches may be used for machine appliqué, including the machine blindstitch and decorative stitches. If the entire raw edge isn't going to be covered with stitches, as it is in the machine satin stitch, it's better to cut the appliqués with a ¼" or ³⁄₁₆" seam allowance and turn the seam allowance under, so the appliqués don't fray. You can use fusible webbing and cut the shapes out of the webbing. Fuse them to the wrong side of the appliqué fabric. When you cut the appliqués, add the seam allowances as you cut. Seam allowances may be pressed around onto the other side of the fusible webbing shape before you fuse the appliqué to the base fabric, or seam allowances may be basted under as you would do for hand appliqué (see details of basting in hand appliqué section).

Hand appliqué

For hand appliqué, trace the appliqué shape onto the right side of the fabric with a washable pencil or other

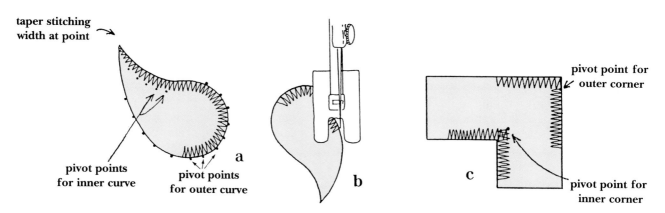

7: Machine appliqué. **a:** *Pivot your fabric around sharp curves, stopping the needle in the appliqué for inside curves at frequent intervals, and on the outside in the base fabric. Narrow the width of your satin stitch as you go into the pointed part of an appliqué.* **b:** *The needle is stopped on the outside edge to pivot on an outer curve. The needle is shown in the left swing of the zigzag satin stitch.* **c:** *Appliqué on a corner, showing pivot points.*

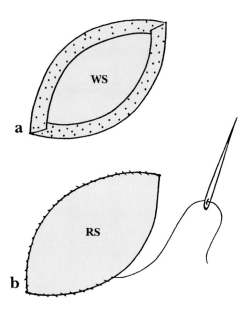

9: Where an appliqué is made of several overlapping pieces, baste the pieces to the background fabric, leaving the seam allowances that will be covered by a second appliqué edge flat (dashed lines).

8: Hand appliqué technique. **a:** *Seam allowances folded to the wrong side of the appliqué.* **b:** *Stitching the appliqué to the background fabric.*

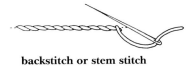
backstitch or stem stitch

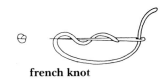
running stitch

french knot

satin stitch

featherstitch

10: Some basic hand embroidery stitches.

nonpermanent marking tool, and cut out the shape, adding ³⁄₁₆″ seam allowances all the way around as you cut. Secure the seam allowances on the wrong side of the appliqué (figure 8a). You may have to make a few cuts (clips) in the seam allowance, perpendicular to the appliqué edge, to get the seam allowance to lie flat, particularly on inward curves. If you clip the seam allowance, be sure you don't go into the appliqué area; stop a few threads before that.

There are many ways to secure the seam allowances, including tacking them in place with a fabric glue stick, using liquid starch, and basting them in place. After the seam allowances are secured, baste the appliqué to the base fabric and stitch it in place, using a very small tacking stitch and hand sewing thread that matches the appliqué fabric as closely as possible (Fig. 8b). Run the hand sewing thread through beeswax before use to keep it from tangling.

Where several appliqué shapes will overlap, the seam allowances that are going to be covered by another appliqué piece should not be turned under (figure 9). Baste the pieces in place on the block before starting to appliqué.

Hand Embroidery

Several projects call for details that are hand embroidered. Embroidery stitches are easy to do; some basic ones are shown in figure 10. Separate 6-strand cotton embroidery floss into the number of strands indicated in the project. Use a size 7 or 8 crewel or embroidery needle, which has a larger eye than a sharp or a be-

tween. Use an embroidery hoop to keep an even tension on your work. When you embroider, do not pull your stitches too tight as you don't want your work to pucker.

Applying Piping and Other Trim

Applying piping or other decorative trim is very simple. For a straight edge, simply lay the piping or lace against the fabric, having the raw edges of the piping or the gathered edge of the lace even with the raw

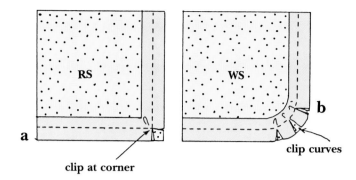

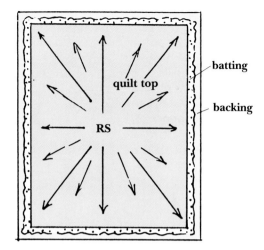

11: Applying piping. **a:** *Basting piping to a rectangular shape.* **b:** *Basting piping to a curve. Clip seam allowances as shown.*

13: Basting the quilt.

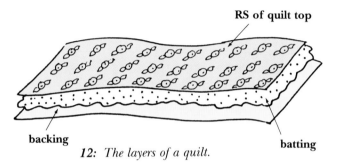

12: The layers of a quilt.

edge of the fabric, and baste it in place using a ¼″ seam allowance.

To pipe a rectangular shape, when you get near the corner, stop stitching ¼″ from the edge. Make a small clip in the seam allowance of the piping, but do not cut through to the area containing the cord itself (figure 11a). Continue basting the trim along the next edge.

To pipe a curved edge, clip into the seam allowance of the trim every ½″ or so to make the trim lie flat (figure 11b). Be careful not to cut past the seam allowance and into the piping itself! Continue basting. The piping is usually permanently sewn in at the same time the two pieces of fabric that it is in between are joined.

Basting the Quilt Layers

Your quilt can be thought of as a sandwich: the "bread" is the backing fabric and the quilt top; the filler is the batting (figure 12). To baste the layers together, tape the backing fabric face-down to your work surface, center the batting over the backing fabric, and center the quilt top over the batting. You can pin-baste or thread baste the three layers together, which will hold them together temporarily while you quilt. To thread-baste, using an easily visible thread, start stitching with very large running stitches in the center of the quilt and work outward, smoothing the

layers as you baste to be sure there are no puckers in the fabric (see figure 13). After you are done quilting, remove the basting. To pin baste, pin through all three layers with small safety pins, pinning every 3 or 4 inches. Try to avoid pinning near where you're going to have to stitch later on.

Machine Quilting Techniques

The model projects in this book have all been machine quilted. You may choose to hand quilt your project if you wish, but since our focus is on speed techniques, we will only discuss the basics of machine quilting here.

To machine quilt, loosen the upper tension of the machine very slightly, and thread the top of the machine with a neutral color all-purpose thread or clear nylon monofilament. Load the bobbin with thread to match color of the backing fabric. Set the machine stitch length to approximately 8 stitches per inch.

For best results, use a walking foot or quilting foot. These normally do not come with your machine as standard equipment, but they can be purchased at a sewing machine store for your particular brand of machine, and they are relatively inexpensive. Such a foot will feed the layers of your quilt together evenly, allowing you to machine quilt without puckers, which you might get if you use a standard foot. When using a standard foot, the feed dogs tend to push the bottom layer of the quilt through faster than you can hand-push the top layers of the fabric, resulting in the puckering.

You may also choose to machine quilt free-motion style. To do this, use a darning foot and lower your feed dogs. You will now have to maneuver the fabric through the machine by hand, but you will able to make curves and swirls, instead of stitching in a straight line. The possibilities here are endless!

For best results, machine quilt around the edges of each appliqué and stitch along all of the seamlines (stitch in the ditch). Stitch again ¼″ from the seamlines and the appliqué edges. If you have chosen batting that needs to be heavily quilted (see the section on batting), you may quilt any open areas with a filler stitch such as criss-crossed lines (figure 14a) or echo quilting, which just means quilting ¼″ from each previous line of quilting around a shape until the area is filled (14b). If your batting doesn't require such heavy quilting, you can space your quilting lines further apart.

a　　　　　　　　　　　　　　　　　　**b**

14: Two quilting patterns. **a:** *Criss-cross quilting lines.* **b:** *Echo quilting.*

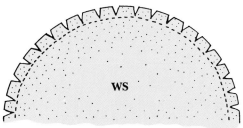

15: Clipping curves.

Clipping Curves and Corners

This terribly important step is often overlooked when making a project, and it results in curved areas that will not lie flat or corners that are rounded when you want them to be square. Clipping the curves of the seam allowances of a rounded project (figure 15) will give you a nice, flat curved edge, and it will also eliminate the bulk of the seam allowance in a project. This neatens its appearance and makes it easier to quilt as well. You certainly wouldn't want an oval placemat that curls towards your place setting, or one with bulky edges.

Clipping the corners off the seam allowances of a rectangular project (figure 16) reduces the bulk at the corners, allowing the corners to lie flat and have a nicely pointed appearance. Always clip close to but not through the stitching lines.

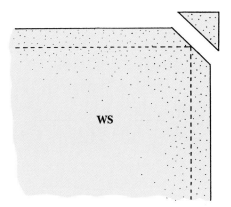

16: Clipping corners.

Making Your Own Binding

I have used prepackaged binding throughout this book. However, you can easily make your own binding, which is sometimes easier than trying to find an exact match to your fabric. To make your own double-fold bias binding, first mark a large square of cloth (such as a yard of cloth) so the lower left and upper right corners are connected by a diagonal line. The diagonal line is the bias of the cloth. The angle between that line and the bottom edge is 45° (figure 17a). (It is also 45° between the diagonal line and the side edge.) Measuring parallel to the diagonal line, mark and cut 2″ wide strips of fabric. All of the strips must have 45° angles at the ends (17b). Stitch the ends of the strips together as shown in the figure 17c to make a long length of bias binding. Keep adding strips until you get the yardage of bias binding you need, as indicated in the materials list of your project. Clip off the little tails of seam allowance after stitching the strips together (17c) and press the seam allowances open. To make the first fold of the tape, fold both sides of the strip so they meet at the center and press (17d). Next, fold the strip down the centerline to make the center fold (17e); this results in a double-fold bias binding (17f). The folded width will be ½″ (¼ of the unfolded width).

Applying the Binding

Binding is done *after you have quilted* and trimmed any extra batting and backing off your quilt. Unfold the

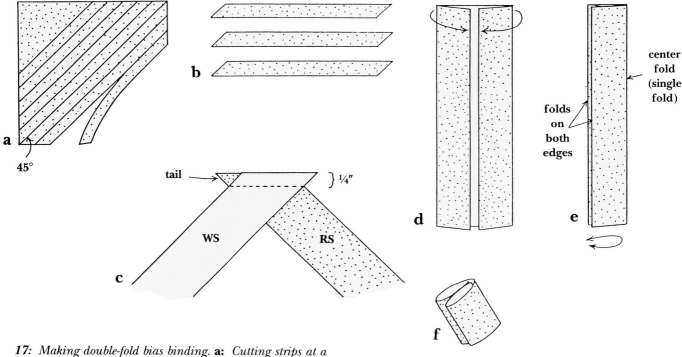

17: Making double-fold bias binding. **a:** *Cutting strips at a 45° angle.* **b:** *The cut strips.* **c:** *Joining two strips.* **d:** *Folding the sides in to meet the center.* **e:** *Folding the strip in half so the two previous folds end up at the left.* **f:** *Cross-section of bias binding.*

bias binding, homemade or purchased, and place one long edge of the binding against the edge of the quilt top, with right sides of the fabric facing and raw edges aligned. Stitch along the top crease of the binding to within ½″ of the quilt's corner (figure 18a). End off the thread. At the corner, fold the binding up, aligning the side of the binding with the side of the quilt (18b). Fold the binding down, having the resulting fold of the binding even with the top edge of the quilt and continue stitching (18c). Repeat the procedure for each side of the quilt and to turn the corners. Fold the loose edge of the binding to the opposite (backing) side of the quilt and hand slipstitch it in place with a ½″ seam allowance turned under, making sure your stitches are not visible on the front of the quilt (18d).

Hanging a Quilt

To hang a quilt as a wall hanging, you can make a fabric tube and attach it to the back side of the quilt near the top. To make one:

1. Cut a strip of fabric 8″ wide: cut the length of the strip 1″ shorter than the width of the quilt. For example, if your quilt is 30 × 30″, your strip would be 8 × 29″.
2. With right sides of fabric facing, fold the tube in half down its length and stitch the two long edges together, ¼″ from the double raw edges (figure 19a). Turn the tube right-side out.
3. Turn in a hem of ¼″ at the ends of the tube and secure them with stitching (19b).
4. Press the tube so that the seam is in the center of the flattened area.
5. Slipstitch the tube to the backing side of the quilt by hand, near the top (19c). Insert a rod in the tube for hanging.
6. Suspend the rod from curtain rod holders, or use thin wires and S-hooks and hang the quilt from a moulding.

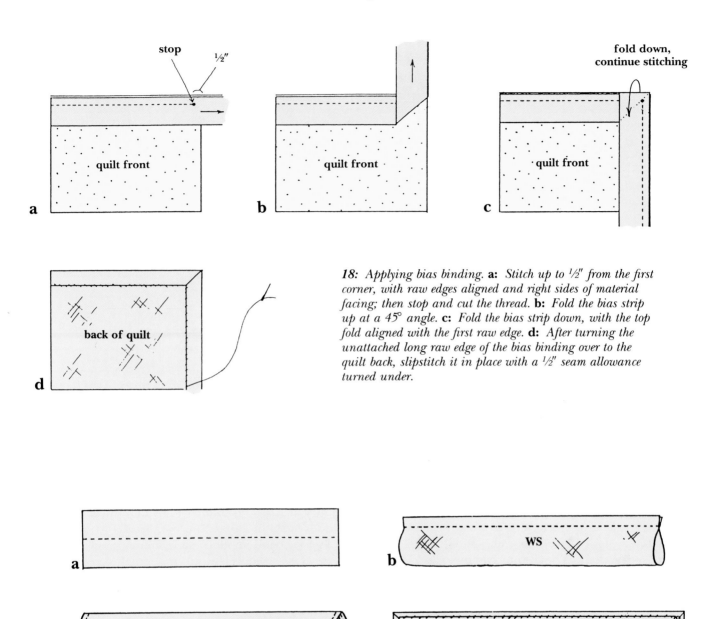

18: Applying bias binding. a: *Stitch up to ½" from the first corner, with raw edges aligned and right sides of material facing; then stop and cut the thread.* **b:** *Fold the bias strip up at a 45° angle.* **c:** *Fold the bias strip down, with the top fold aligned with the first raw edge.* **d:** *After turning the unattached long raw edge of the bias binding over to the quilt back, slipstitch it in place with a ½" seam allowance turned under.*

19: *Making a tube for hanging a quilt.*

Supplies and Tools

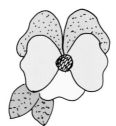

Fabric

I recommend using only 100% cotton fabrics. Cotton is very easy to work with and it will not slide as you stitch, as a blend or a polyester will. Cotton is also very forgiving if you happen to make a mistake. Blends may be used when necessary, but make sure they have a higher percentage of cotton than of the other fibers. Blends have a tendency to slip and slide, or to fray when washing, so always try to use cotton.

Prewash and press all fabrics before beginning a project. Swish around a test swatch of each fabric in warm water and see if it bleeds or crocks (loses its dye into the washwater). Replace any fabrics that aren't colorfast, as the dye may spoil your completed project when it is laundered later on. Prewashing removes any sizing or starchy finishes that are added to the fabric by the manufacturers, which makes the fabric easier to handle, and allows the fabric to shrink *before* you start your project.

Be sure your fabrics are on grain after they are washed (see figure 20). If you cut rectangular pieces when the fabric is off grain, the pieces are more likely to stretch out of shape while you're working with them, because the bias is stretchier than the straight grain of the fabric. (It's not necessary to use the straight grain for appliqués, however.)

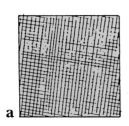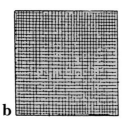

20: *Off-grain fabric and on-grain fabric.*

Thread

I prefer to use all-purpose thread (cotton-wrapped polyester) for piecing and quilting my projects. However, I like to use special threads such as rayon or metallic thread for machine appliqué. Rayon and metallics, however, are purely decorative and should not be used for any assembly work. You may also use 100% cotton thread, but you'll have a better range of colors to choose from if you opt for all-purpose thread. For hand appliqué, try to get 100% cotton hand sewing thread, which is a bit thinner than all-purpose thread and so is less noticeable. Run the thread through beeswax for hand appliqué so it doesn't tangle easily. For hand embroidery, the embroidery floss recommended is 6-strand 100% cotton floss, or pearl cotton, whichever is noted in the individual project. Separate a piece of floss into individual strands, and use the number of strands indicated in the project instructions. This will take the twist out of the floss and allow your stitches to lie flat.

Batting

I have used traditional-weight polyester batting or polyester fleece in the projects in this book. It is the most commonly available form of batting. When purchasing batting for a machine-made project, always read the package carefully. You will notice that the manufacturer gives recommendations as to the spaces between lines of quilting; this is very important! If you plan to do a minimal amount of quilting, choose a batting with a wider spacing ratio. If not, your batting will shift when you wash the finished item and it could become a lumpy mess. Also, do not choose a high loft or "fat" batting for hand or machine quilting. These are meant for tied quilts and are very difficult to quilt through.

Quilt batting is normally sold by the precut piece in a bag, or by the yard from a bolt. Fleece, which is a very dense form of polyester batting, is sold by the yard and should be used for placemats and runners, as it gives the finished piece a bit more stiffness than regular batting would.

Fusible Webbing

Fusible transfer webbing is used in the projects to bond appliqués to the background fabric of the quilt top prior to machine appliqué. (It isn't needed for hand appliqué.) When a project calls for fusible webbing, choose a paper-backed nonwoven webbing that becomes sticky on both sides when it is pressed with an iron. (Read the instructions from the manufacturer to see how hot to make your iron.) Fusible webbing goes by various brand names, and it may be sold by the yard or in prepackaged units at fabric stores. Most webbing sold by the yard is 18″ wide. Choose a lightweight webbing to go with the lightweight fabrics that you will be using. (It is difficult to quilt through heavy webbing.) See the section on appliqué basics for instructions on using fusible transfer webbing.

Stabilizer

Stabilizer is an extra layer of lightweight paper or nonwoven fabric that is placed under your base fabric, giving the base fabric extra body and stability, while you do machine appliqué. If you've ever attempted machine appliqué and have become discouraged because your fabric became tangled in the hole in the throat plate of your machine, you will be glad to know help is on the way: Stabilizer will prevent this from happening. Stabilizer is sold in fabric stores, by the yard or prepackaged. Get the tear-away kind, so the excess around the appliqué can be torn off when you are through machine-stitching your appliqué. You may also use scratch paper such as tracing paper as stabilizer. Pin a piece of stabilizer to the wrong side of the base fabric at the corners. The stabilizer should be cut slightly larger than the piece of base fabric you're working on. Then do your machine appliqué work.

The Sewing Machine

Always keep your sewing machine in good working condition—especially if you plan to do any machine appliqué! Your sewing machine is like any other machine, whether it be your car or your videocassette recorder: It needs to be cleaned and serviced once in awhile. Regularly clean and oil your machine. Cleaning removes the debris that can clog the feed dogs or jam the machine. Oiling keeps the machine running smoothly and *quietly*. A noisy machine is one in need of help! Referring to your owner's manual, adjust the thread tension properly. The tension must be evenly balanced! I've run across many students' machines that have had their bobbin tension tightened to the point where it cannot be loosened except with great difficulty. If, after you try to adjust your bobbin tension, you are still having trouble, adjust the tension as follows:

1. Hold the bobbin case in your hand and slide the bobbin into it, threading the bobbin as if it were in the machine. Then let go of the case while holding onto end of the bobbin thread. If the case slides down to the floor, leaving you with a 4-foot tail of thread, your tension is too loose.
2. If not, gently shake the thread and watch the bobbin case: if it doesn't go anywhere, your tension is much too tight! If it slips ever so slightly, you have nearly perfect tension.
3. Now, replace the bobbin case and bobbin in the machine, and thread the machine with the same weight of thread used in the bobbin, but in a different color. Test-sew a length of straight stitch on a doubled scrap of fabric and look at the resulting stitch. If the bobbin thread has been pulled to the top of the fabric, your upper tension is too tight. If the upper thread is pulled to the bottom side of the folded fabric, your upper tension is too loose.
4. Adjust the upper tension so that the stitch becomes balanced.

If you have tried the steps given above and the tension is still awful, have it professionally serviced. It's worth it! You wouldn't neglect a tuneup on your car, would you?

Rotary Cutters, Mats, and Rulers

Rotary Cutter: A rotary cutter is a sharp circular blade with a handle; some blades are protected by a cover, which moves up when you press down, exposing the blade. A rotary cutter is a big time-saver when it comes to cutting. These things are a quilter's dream come true! The projects in this book can be cut with a ro-

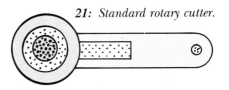

21: Standard rotary cutter.

tary cutter, except for the appliqués, which require scissors. Rotary cutters now come in a variety of shapes and sizes, and some even have double blades for cutting precise strips. However, I recommend a single-blade large cutter. Smaller cutters require a bit more work on your part. When choosing a rotary cutter, pick the one that feels the most comfortable in your hand. If you suffer from arthritis, try a cutter with a curved handle for a more natural grip. If possible, try some friends' cutters before buying to see which brand and size you like best. Replacement blades can be purchased when yours gets dull. If the rotary cutter skips along the fabric as you cut, it is probably nicked, and you need a new blade. ALWAYS cut away from you, and keep cutters, pins and any other sharp tools out of the reach of children. See the general directions section for "how to" advice on rotary cutting.

Do not attempt to cut with a rotary blade if you do not have a rotary cutting mat! I have watched as quilters have attempted to cut on cardboard or other surfaces—what a mess! Purchase a rotary cutting mat with a gridded measuring surface. Many sizes are available, but a 24″ × 36″ size is quite comfortable and large enough for most projects. Purchase a mat that is "self-healing," meaning the mat will not retain the deep grooves that are cut into it: the grooves sort of "disappear," rather than leaving an uneven cutting surface.

Rulers for rotary cutting: There are a wide variety of rulers available for use with rotary cutters and mats. All are made of clear plastic with measurement and sometimes angle markings. For the most versatile ruler, use the 6″ × 24″ size. However, for smaller jobs you may wish to use a smaller ruler. For cutting squares and triangles, triangular and square rotary cutting rulers are also available. To keep your ruler from slipping as you cut, you can secure sandpaper squares or dots on the wrong side of the ruler. The ruler should be fairly thick, so the fabric, if folded several thicknesses, is still held against it when you cut. If you hit the side of a metal ruler with a rotary cutter, you may damage the blade, which is why a plastic ruler is preferable.

Scissors

Always use a nice sharp pair of scissors for cutting fabric, and use them only for this purpose. Tag them FABRIC ONLY and use an older pair of scissors for cutting paper or plastic. Occasionally, the nonquilters in your environment will try to use your fabric scissors for cutting paper or whatever. Discourage them from doing this by putting out *alternate scissors* for them to use, and keep your fabric scissors tucked away when

you're not using it for cutting fabric. Your scissors should not cause you any discomfort when you cut. If it does, you may need to have them sharpened and the joint oiled.

Marking Pens and Pencils

Always use water-soluble pens or pencils for marking fabrics. DO NOT use a #2 graphite pencil for marking fabric. Fabric and quilting supply stores carry a large number of water-soluble marking instruments, including pencils specially designed for quilters. You can also use tailor's chalk or a soap sliver. You can buy quilter's pencils in different colors. Use a white, yellow or silver pencil for marking on dark fabrics, or use a blue, black, or silver pencil for marking on light-colored fabric.

When in doubt, test your marking tool on a scrap of fabric and wash the fabric before you use it to mark the real thing. It should wash away easily.

Seam Ripper

No, I'm not a perfect stitcher either, so I always have several of these little wonders handy. Using one doesn't mean you can't stitch well—it means that you care enough about what you're doing to do it properly! Seam rippers tend to get dull after repeated use. Replace them as necessary. It's better to rip than to have a crooked quilt.

Other Useful Items

Here are some other tools and supplies you'll probably need.

- Sewing machine needles (size 9 or 11 universal point for appliqué work and piecing)
- Straight pins
- Tracing paper
- Graph paper for enlarging patterns
- Colored pencils for planning alternate color combinations of quilt designs
- Embroidery thread for hand embroidery (see individual project's materials list for specifics)
- Embroidery needles
- Masking tape for tagging parts of quilts, etc., before they are assembled
- An iron

See the materials list of your project for any other items specific to that project.

Village Streets Lap Quilt

Reminiscent of New England row houses, this charming quilt works up in a flash. Because there are no bias edges or triangle pieces to worry about, it is an excellent project for a beginner. Change the colors of the houses to suit your own decor, but try to use a nice floral fabric for the borders. Finished size: 40 × 52″.

Materials

- ⅓ yard EACH of fabric in 3 colors for the houses: medium blue, medium teal, and medium pink in the model

- 4½″ × 33″ strip in each of 3 roof colors: mustard, medium rose, and light blue in the model

- ¼ yard of pale green print fabric for the horizontal ''grass'' rows

- ⅔ yard black fabric for the windows, doors, and inner border

- 2½ × 24″ strip of brick red solid fabric for the chimneys

- ⅓ yard tan fabric for the chimney rows

- 1½ yards of a coordinating floral print fabric for the outer border

- 42 × 54″ piece of quilt batting

- 42 × 54″ piece of backing fabric of choice

- 5½ yards of black double-fold quilt binding (folded width, ½″; unfolded width, 2″)

- All-purpose sewing thread in a neutral color and black

Directions

All construction is done right sides of fabric facing and seam allowances of ¼″, which are included in the given measurements.

1. Cut your fabric strips as indicated in the cutting guides for each fabric.
2. Look at the quilt construction diagram, 1–1, and the house construction diagram 1–2, to familiarize yourself with the parts of the project.
3. First we'll make the window units (AWA) of the house. Take one black 2½ × 17″ strip and two 1½ × 17″ strips of the first house color (we'll call it house color 1). Referring to figure 1–3, seam them together on a long side to make an AWA strip and cut across all three strips to make 2½″-wide AWA window units. Make 6 AWA window units with house color 1. Set them aside.
4. Repeat step 3 with house colors 2 and 3. Set the AWA units aside.

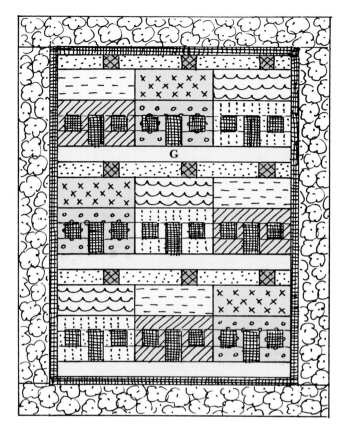

1–1: *Construction diagram of the quilt.*

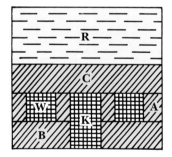

1–2: *Construction diagram of a house block.*

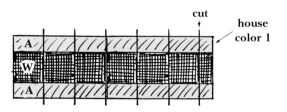

1–3: *Cutting the AWA window units.*

Quantity and Size   *Use*

Black fabric cutting guide

Three	2½ × 17″	windows (W)
One	2½ × 30″	doors (K)
Two	1½ × 42½″	inner border
Two	1½ × 30½″	inner border

Floral border fabric cutting guide

| Two | 4½ × 40½″ | top/bottom outer border |
| Two | 4½ × 44½″ | side outer border |

From each house color* cut

Two	1½ × 17″	A pieces
One	2½ × 30″	B pieces
One	2½ × 33″	C pieces

Tan fabric cutting guide

| One | 8½ × 24″ | E and H pieces |
| One | 2½ × 8″ | F squares |

Pale green print cutting guide

| Three | 2½ × 30½″ | G strips |

*Medium blue, medium teal, and medium pink floral in the model.

5. Take the 2½ × 30″ strip of house color 1 and cut it into six 2½ × 4½″ B pieces. Do the same for house color 2 and house color 3.

6. Stitch a B piece on its long side below each AWA unit, as shown in figure 1–4, to make an AWA + B unit. The A and B pieces should be of the same color within the same unit. Do this for all eighteen AWA units. Set them aside.

7. Take the 2½ × 30″ black strip and cut six 2½ × 4½″ doors (K) from it.

8. On both long sides of a K piece (door), sew an AWA + B unit (see figure 1–5). The two AWA + B pieces that are on either side of one door should be of the same house color. The unit formed is the windows + door unit. Repeat eight more times. Set the units aside.

1–4: *B piece stitched below an AWA window unit.*

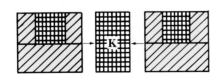

1–5: *Joining two AWA window units to a door (K).*

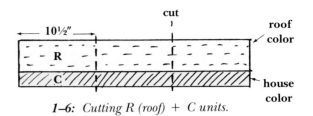

1–6: *Cutting R (roof) + C units.*

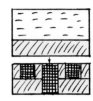

1–7: *Joining an RC unit to a windows + door unit to make a house block.*

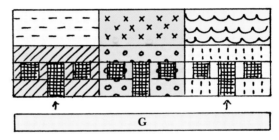

1–8: *G strip stitched to the bottom of a house row.*

9. Take the 2½ × 33″ piece of fabric of house color 1 and the 4½ × 33″ strip of the roof fabric that goes with that house color (see photo). Seam them together on one long side. Then cut across a 2-strip unit to make three 10½″-wide RC units from house color 1, as shown in figure 1–6. Repeat for the other two roof strips and the other two 2½ × 33″ strips of house color fabric (house colors 2 and 3).

10. Take each RC unit and match it up with the windows + door unit from step 8 that has the same house color as C. Stitch the RC piece to the windows + door unit as shown in figure 1–7 to make a house block. Repeat for a total of 9 house blocks.

11. Referring to the color photo for placement if necessary, stitch 3 of the house blocks together along their sides to form a house row. Press. Stitch one pale green 2½ × 30½″ G strip to the bottom of each house row (figure 1–8). Press the seam allowances towards the G strip. Repeat for the other two house rows. Set them aside.

12. Take your 8½ × 24″ piece of tan fabric and your 2½ × 24″ strip of brick red fabric for the chimneys. Seam them together on a long side and slice across the two strips to make nine 2½″ wide ED units as shown in figure 1–9a. Trim three of them so the tan side becomes 6½″ (see figure 1–9b); the trimmed ones are now DH units.

13. Cut three 2½ × 2½″ F squares from the tan 2½ × 8″ strip. Then stitch a DH unit to two ED units and an F square to make a chimney row, as shown in

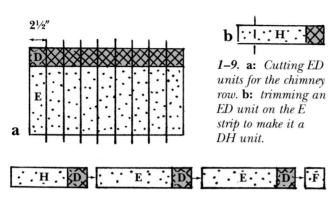

a

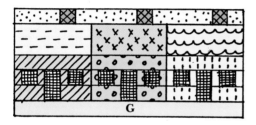

b

1–9. **a:** *Cutting ED units for the chimney row.* **b:** *trimming an ED unit on the E strip to make it a DH unit.*

1–10: Stitching together the pieces to form a chimney row.

1–11: A house + chimney row.

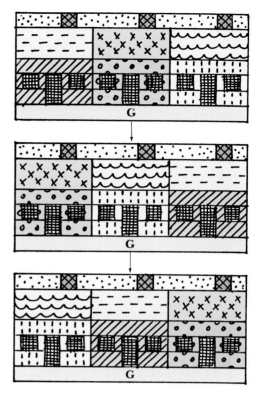

1–12: Assembling the quilt center.

figure 1–10. Make two more chimney rows the same way and press the seam allowances towards the darker fabric.

14. Stitch one chimney row to the top edge of each house row + G strip from step 11. Press the seam allowances towards the chimney rows (figure 1–11).

15. Stitch the 3 house + chimney row units made in step 14 together to form the quilt center (figure 1–12). Press.

16. See figure 1–13 for all border attachment steps. Stitch one 42½″ black border strip to the left and one to the right side of your quilt center. Stitch one 32½″ black border strip to the top and one to the bottom of the quilt center.

17. Stitch one 44½ × 4½″ floral border strip to the left and one to the right of the quilt center made in step 16. Stitch one 4½ × 40½″ floral border strip to the top and one to the bottom of the quilt. This completes the quilt top.

18. Tape the quilt back to your work surface, wrong side up, center the batting over the backing, and center the quilt top right-side up over the batting. Hand-baste or pin-baste the layers together. Referring to the general directions, hand or machine quilt it as desired.

19. After quilting, baste around the outside edges of the quilt top, about ¼″ in from the raw edges, and trim away the excess batting and backing fabric that extend beyond the quilt top to prepare the quilt for the binding.

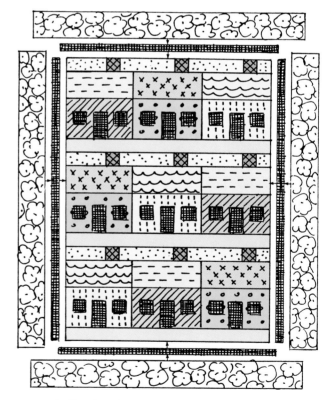

1–13: Attaching borders to the quilt center.

20. Bind the quilt with the bias binding, using black thread; see general directions for more binding information.

Pansy Patch Wall Hanging

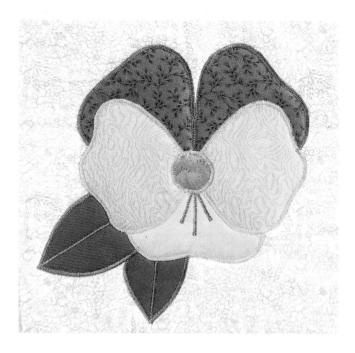

Materials

- ⅓ yard off-white print fabric for the blocks
- ⅓ yard medium yellow print fabric (inner border, petals)
- ⅓ yard solid dark green fabric (inner border, leaves)
- ¼ yard of pale yellow solid fabric (petals)
- 6 × 6″ scrap of deep orange for flower centers
- ½ yard of deep purple print fabric (outer border and petals)
- 17 × 18″ piece of paper-backed fusible transfer webbing (for machine appliqué only)
- All-purpose sewing threads to match all of the fabrics
- Hand sewing threads to match the fabrics (for hand appliqué only)
- Four 9 × 9″ pieces of tear-away stabilizer (for machine appliqué; see general directions)
- 4 yards of dark green double-fold quilt binding (folded width ½″; unfolded width 2″)
- 30 × 30″ piece of backing fabric
- 30 × 30″ piece of low-loft quilt batting or fleece

If you've always been hesitant about trying satin-stitch machine appliqué, don't be! It's a quick and fun way to appliqué just about any motif! Just be sure to use a stabilizer under your work to keep the needle from shoving the fabric through the hole in the throat plate of your machine and you won't have any difficulty stitching. (If you wish, you may do hand appliqué instead, however.) Finished size of the wall hanging: 28 × 28″; block size, 9″ × 9″.

Directions

Construction is done right sides of fabric facing and seam allowances of ¼″, which are included in all of the given measurements. Appliqué patterns are given without seam allowances. (If you are doing machine appliqué, the appliqué pieces do not require seam allowances.) Steps that pertain to machine appliqué only are marked with an M. Steps that pertain to hand appliqué only are marked with an H. For hand appliqué, add ³⁄₁₆″ seam allowances around each appliqué piece before cutting and see the hand appliqué instructions in the general directions section of the book.

1. From the purple fabric cut two 3½ × 22½″ strips and two 3½ × 28½″ strips. Set these aside for the outer borders.

2. From the dark green fabric cut two 2½ × 45″ strips. Repeat with the medium yellow print fabric. Cut two 2½″ squares from the end of one medium yellow strip and two from the green strip. Set the strips and squares aside. These will become the checkered borders.

3. From the off-white print fabric cut four 9½″ squares for the background fabric of the blocks. Fold each square into quarters and press. The creases will mark your center lines. Trace the entire appliqué pattern, centered, on the front of each square, using a washable pencil or chalk, as a placement guide.

4M. *For machine appliqué,* trace the complete reversed appliqué pattern onto the paper side of the fusible webbing. Do this 4 times. Carefully cut each tracing apart into its individual webbing pieces, and fuse each webbing piece to the wrong side of the correct fabric: Fuse the lower petal sections to the pale yellow solid, the middle petal sections to the medium yellow print, the upper petal sections to the purple fabric, the flower centers to the scrap of deep orange fabric, and the leaf sections to the green fabric.

4H. *For hand appliqué,* trace out each individual leaf, petal, or flower center onto template cardboard and cut each out of the cardboard to make templates. Label the right side of each template. Trace 4 of each appliqué template, unreversed, to the front of the fabric needed for that appliqué piece, leaving enough room for ³⁄₁₆″ seam allowances around each piece. For example, trace the leaves onto the front of the dark

a

b

2–1. **a:** *For machine appliqué, fuse the appliqués, centered, on each block.* **b:** *For hand appliqué, baste the pieces to the block, leaving the seam allowances that are overlapped by another appliqué piece flat (dashed lines).*

green fabric; trace the upper petals onto the front of the purple fabric.

5. Cut out all of the appliqué pieces from their fabrics (for hand appliqué only, add ³⁄₁₆″ seam allowances as you cut). Transfer the embroidery markings indicated by dashed lines to the 4 pale yellow lower petal sections on the front of the fabric. Transfer the dashed markings to the leaves also.

6M. Using the traced appliqué patterns on the block as guidelines, peel the paper off the fusible webbing, arrange one set of appliqués on each of the off-white background blocks (figure 2–1a), and fuse them in place with a warm iron. Then pin a piece of tear-away stabilizer to the back (wrong side) of each of the four blocks.

6H. Secure the seam allowances of your appliqué pieces at the back of each piece (see general instructions) except where another pattern piece will overlap; in those places leave the seam allowance unturned (figure 2–1b). Using the complete appliqué patterns you previously drew on the blocks as a guide, arrange and baste one set of appliqués to each of the off-white blocks.

7M. Machine appliqué all of the pieces in place using a medium-width machine satin stitch, with thread that matches the fabric in the bobbin and the needle. Change threads as necessary to match each appliqué.

7H. Using hand sewing thread close in color to the piece to be attached, hand appliqué each piece in place, starting with the ones that are the closest to the block fabric (the leaves and the purple petals).

8. Satin stitch along the dashed embroidery lines on the lower petals, using the purple thread. Stitch along the centers of the leaves with the green thread on the dashed lines.

9. To assemble the blocks, with right sides of fabric facing, stitch the four blocks together to make the quilt center (figure 2–2); press it; and set it aside.

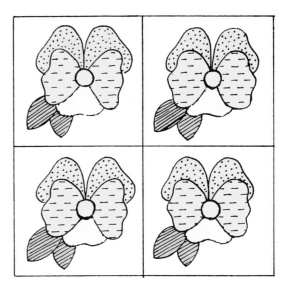

2–2: The 4 appliquéd blocks, stitched together to form the quilt center.

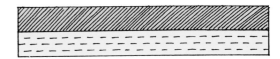

2–3: A green and a yellow strip, stitched together on a long side.

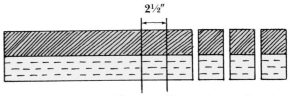

2½″

2–4: Cut eighteen 2½″-wide yellow-and-green A units.

10. Stitch together one 2½ × 40″ medium yellow strip and one green strip the same size on one long side; repeat with the second medium yellow and green strip (figure 2–3). Press the seam allowances towards the green fabric.

11. Cutting across the two-color strip you just made, cut eighteen 2½″ wide 2-square yellow-and-green rectangles (which we will call A units), as shown in figure 2–4. You will have extra fabric.

12. To make the side inner border, stitch together four A units, as shown in figure 2–5a. Add a medium yellow 2½″ square, cut in step 2, to the purple end of the strip (see 2–5a). Make another side inner border the same way. Set them aside. To make the top inner border, stitch five A units together as shown in figure 2–5b. Add a green 2½″ square to the yellow end of the top inner border (see 2–5b). Make another pieced strip the same way for the bottom inner border.

13. Stitch the side inner border strips to either side of the quilt center. Stitch the top inner border to the top

2–5: Inner borders. **a:** Piece a side inner border from four yellow-and-green rectangles and an extra yellow square. **b:** Piece the top and bottom inner borders from five yellow-and-green A units plus one extra green square.

of the quilt center and the bottom inner border to the bottom of the quilt center, as shown in figure 2–6.

14. To attach the outer borders, stitch one 3½ × 22½″ purple strip to the top of the quilt center and one to the bottom, as shown in figure 2–7. Stitch one 3½ × 28½″ purple strip to each side of the quilt center. Press the seam allowances towards the purple border strips.

15. Tape the quilt backing to your work surface, face down, center the batting over it, and center the quilt top, face up, over that. Hand-baste or pin-baste the layers together.

16. Referring to the general directions, hand or machine quilt your project as you wish.

17. After quilting, baste about ¼″ in from the raw edges, all around the quilt top. Trim away any excess batting and backing fabric that extends beyond the quilt top.

18. Bind the quilt with the double-fold binding, referring to the general directions if necessary. Stitch the binding in place with the green thread to complete the quilt.

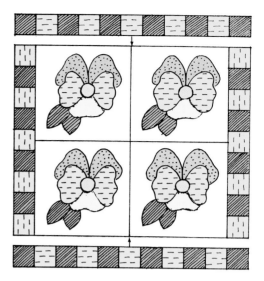

2–6: Sew the shorter inner borders to the sides of the quilt top and the longer inner borders to the top and bottom of the quilt top.

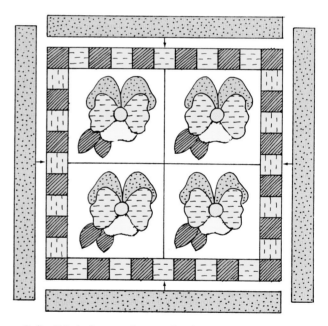

2–7: Stitch the purple outer borders to the quilt center, attaching the shorter borders first.

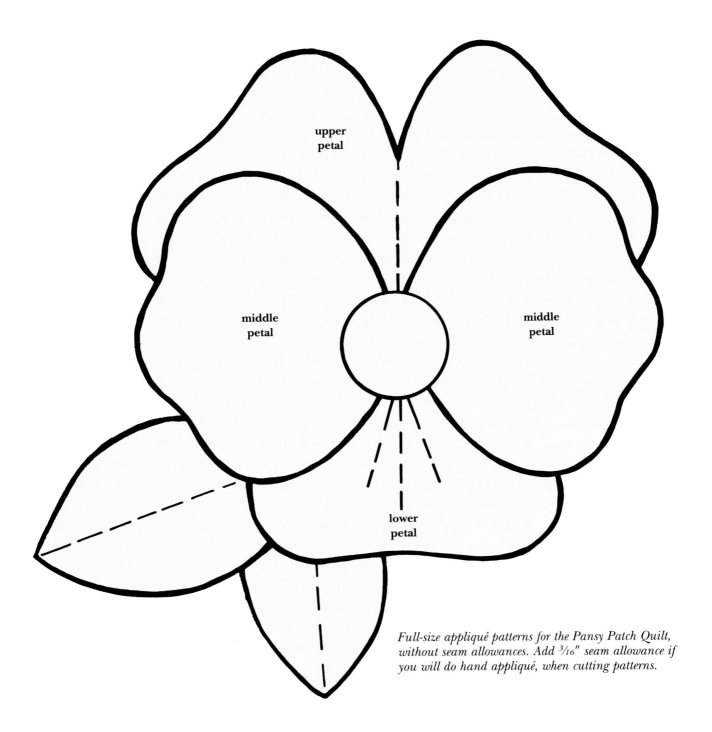

Full-size appliqué patterns for the Pansy Patch Quilt, without seam allowances. Add ³⁄₁₆" seam allowance if you will do hand appliqué, when cutting patterns.

Squawking Chickens Lap or Wall Quilt

Four perky chickens make this wall quilt worth squawking about. Hang it in or near your kitchen and you could find yourself craving a nice chicken dinner! I used a barnyard print fabric for the borders to give it just the right touch. Finished size, 42 × 46″; block size, 16 × 18″.

Green print barnyard fabric cutting guide

Quantity and Size		Use
Two	2½ × 38½″	border
Two	2½ × 46½″	border

Medium red print fabric cutting guide

Quantity and Size		Use
Six	2½ × 16½″	short sashing strips (N)
Three	2½ × 42½	long sashing strips (M)*

*Cut these first.

Tan print fabric cutting guide

Quantity and Size		Use
Four	2½ × 10½″	A pieces
Eight	2½ × 2½″	B squares
Eight	4½ × 6½″	C pieces
Eight	2½ × 4½″	D pieces
Four	2½ × 16½″	row 5
Two	6 × 6″	for units 1 and 2
Four	2½ × 6½″	L pieces

White fabric cutting guide

Quantity and Size		Use
Four	4½ × 4½″	E squares
Eight	2½ × 4½″	F pieces
Eight	2½ × 6½″	G pieces
Twelve	2½ × 2½″	H squares

Small medium green print fabric cutting guide

Quantity and Size		Use
Four	2½ × 16½″	Row 6

Medium yellow print fabric

Quantity and Size		Use
Four	2½ × 4½″	I pieces
Four	2½ × 6½″	J pieces
Four	2½ × 8½″	K pieces

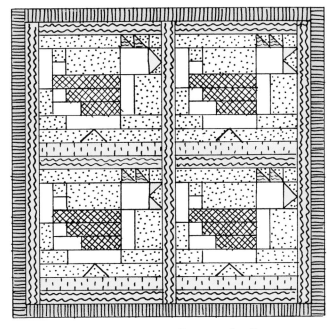

3–1: Construction diagram of quilt.

Materials

- ½ yard of medium red print fabric (for sashing)
- 1½ yards of barnyard print fabric or other green landscape print (for border)
- ½ yard solid white fabric (for chickens)
- ¼ yard medium yellow print fabric (for chickens)
- One 6 × 6″ scrap of dark red fabric (for combs)
- One 6″ × 6″ scrap of orange fabric (for beaks)
- 1 yard tan print fabric (background of blocks)
- ¼ yard medium green print fabric in a small pattern (grass row)
- 44 × 48″ piece of quilt batting
- 44 × 48″ piece of backing fabric
- 5 yards of yellow double-fold quilt binding (folded width, ½″; unfolded width, 2″)
- All-purpose sewing threads in off-white, yellow, and orange
- Four ¾″-diameter black buttons for eyes (or a skein of black embroidery thread)

Directions

Construction is done with right sides of fabric facing and seam allowances of ¼″, which are included in the given measurements. The quilt center is made of 4 blocks, separated by sashing (see construction diagram, figure 3–1). Each individual block is made up

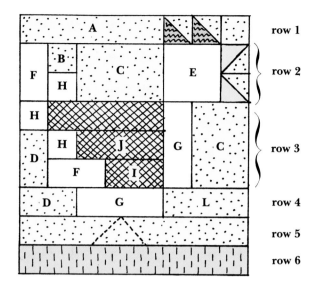

3–2: *Construction diagram of block with open-beaked chicken.*

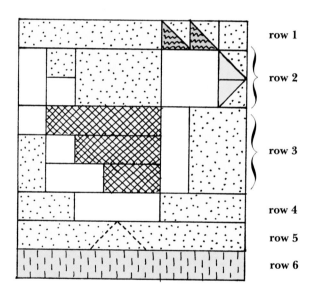

3–3: *Construction diagram of block with closed-beaked chicken.*

of 6 rows; see block construction diagrams, figures 3–2 and 3–3.

1. Cut the indicated quantities and sizes of pieces as listed in the cutting guides.

2. Next, we'll make the unit 1 squares (two-triangle red-tan squares) for the chickens' combs by a speed method. Take one dark red and one tan 6″ square of fabric. On the wrong side of the tan square, mark four 2⅞″ squares. Mark a diagonal line through each square to divide it in half. Pin the tan fabric square and the red fabric square together, right sides facing, with the marked lines facing up. Stitch ¼″ from each side of the diagonal lines, as shown in figure 3–4a.

Closeup of a block.

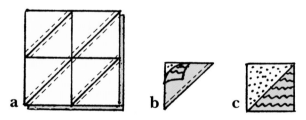

3–4: *Making unit 1 two-triangle squares.* **a:** *Marking and stitching.* **b:** *Cutting the units apart.* **c:** *The completed unit 1.*

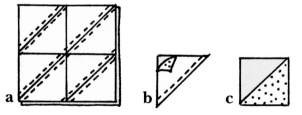

3–5: *Making unit 2 two-triangle squares.* **a:** *Marking and stitching.* **b:** *Cutting the units apart.* **c:** *The completed unit 2.*

After stitching, cut the squares apart along the marked lines (3–4b), and cut each square in half along the marked diagonal line. Press the resulting two-triangle unit 1 squares open (figure 3–4c). You will have 8 of these squares.

3. Next, make 2-triangle orange-tan squares as you did in step 2, but use one 6″ tan square and one 6″ orange square (see figure 3–5). You will thus make

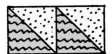

3–6: Stitch two of unit 1 together to form a comb.

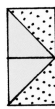

3–7: Stitch two of unit 2 together to form a closed beak (left). Positioned differently (right), two more can form an open beak.

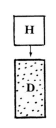

3–10: Piecing the left side of row three.

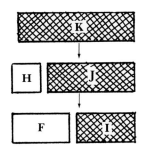

3–11: Piecing the center section of row three.

eight unit 2 squares. We will use them for the beaks.

4. Stitch two of unit 1 together as shown in figure 3–6. This makes the chicken's comb. Make 4 combs. Press them and set them aside.

5. Stitch two of unit 2 together to make an open-mouthed beak (figure 3–7, right) and a closed-mouth beak (3–7 left). Make one more of each beak the same way. Press.

Row Assembly

Now we can assemble the rows to make the blocks. We will need 4 of each row. Refer to figures 3–2 and 3–3 for guidance throughout the assembly.

6. To make row one, stitch together one 2½ × 10½″ tan A piece, one comb (made in step 4), and one 2½″ tan B square as shown in figure 3–8. Make 3 more of row one, press them, and set them aside.

7. To make row two, stitch together one tan B square and one 2½″ white H square on one side to make a 2-square unit. Then, referring to figure 3–9, pin together the 2-square unit, one white F piece (2½ × 4½″), one 4½″ white E square, one tan C piece (4½ × 6½″), and one open beak unit, and stitch them together to make row 2. Make one more of row two with the open beak section and two more with the closed beak sections, press them, and set them aside.

8. To make the left side of row three, stitch one

white H square to one 2½ × 4½″ tan D piece as shown in figure 3–10. Make 3 more units the same way. Press them and set them aside.

9. Refer to figure 3–11 for assembling the center of row three. Stitch one yellow J strip (2½ × 6½″) to a white H square to make an HJ unit. Set it aside. Stitch one yellow I strip (2½ × 4½″) to one white F piece of the same size to make an FI unit. Stitch the HJ unit to the FI unit, and stitch one yellow K piece (2½ × 8½″), as shown in figure 3–11. Make three more row 3 centers the same way, press them, and set them aside.

10. To make the right side of row three (figure 3–12), stitch one white 2½ × 6½″ G piece to one tan 4½ × 6½″ C piece, as shown. Make three more units the same way; press them and set them aside.

11. The assembled row three is shown in figure 3–13. Stitch the left, center, and right sections of row three together to complete the row. Make 4 of these rows; press them and set them aside.

12. To make row 4, stitch together one tan 2½ × 4½″

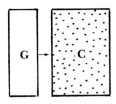

3–12: Piecing the right section of row three.

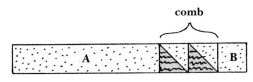

3–8: Row one, showing the placement of the comb.

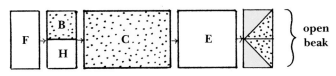

open beak

3–9: Diagram for piecing row two.

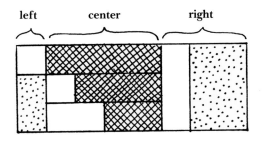

left center right

3–13: The completed row three.

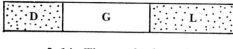

3–14: The completed row 4.

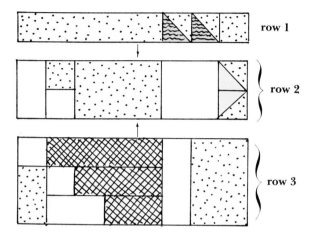

3–15: Stitching rows one through three (the top of the block) for the close-beaked chicken. The same is done for the open-beaked chicken.

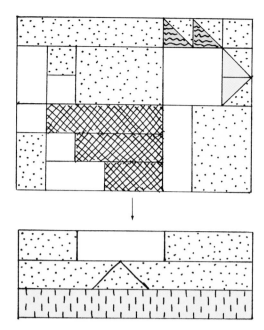

3–17: Joining the upper and lower block section.

D piece, one white 2½ × 6½" G piece and one tan 2½ × 6½" L piece as shown in figure 3–14. Make 3 more of row 4; press them and set them aside. Row 5 is a 2½ × 16 ½" tan strip. Row 6 is a strip the same size of the small green print fabric.

13. To assemble the blocks, stitch together the first three rows to make the upper block section as shown in figure 3–15. Repeat for all four blocks. Set them aside.

14. Stitch rows 4 through 6 together to make the lower block section as shown in figure 3–16. Make three more lower block sections the same way. Press. To complete the block, stitch a lower block section to an upper block section (figure 3–17); make 3 more blocks and press them.

15. For the chicken's legs, in row five mark an inverted V that is centered under the white strip in

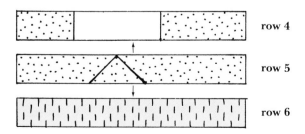

3–16: Stitching rows four through six (the lower block section).

row four (see figure 3–2 for reference). Machine satin-stitch along this inverted V with orange thread, using a wide satin stitch. For added depth, satin stitch again over the first line of stitching to give the legs a raised, dimensional appearance.

16. Referring to figure 3–18, stitch a unit of two blocks and three red print 2½ × 16½" horizontal sashing strips (M) together as shown, with the open-beaked chicken on the bottom. Make a second two-block unit with the open beaked chicken on the top instead (see figure 3–1 for reference). Press.

17. Assemble the quilt by stitching 2½ × 42½" red print N strips to the left and right of the quilt center and between the two 2-block rows (see figure 3–19). Then take one 2½ × 38" green barnyard print border strip and stitch it to the top of the quilt center. Stitch the second one to the bottom of the quilt center. Then stitch a 2½ × 46½" barnyard print border strip to one side of the quilt center and another to the other side. Press. This completes the quilt top.

Basting, Quilting, and Binding

18. Tape the quilt backing to your work surface, face down. Center the batting over the backing and the quilt top, face up, over the batting. Hand-baste or pin-baste the layers together. Referring to the general directions, hand or machine quilt as desired.

19. To prepare the quilt for the binding, baste all around the quilt top, about ¼" in from the raw edge. Trim away the excess batting and backing.

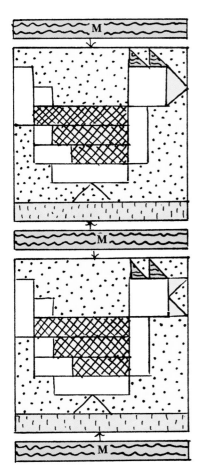

3–18: Stitching the short sashing strips to two blocks.

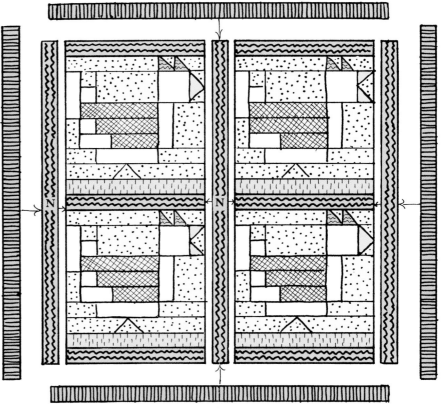

3–19: Stitching on the long sashing strips and the borders.

20. Bind the edges of the quilt with the bias binding, using matching green thread.

21. Stitch one black button to each chicken block for an eye (see photo for reference). If the quilt is for a small child, embroider the eyes in black embroidery thread instead.

Scandinavian Woods Quilt and Runner

This quick-to-make set would be a lovely Christmas gift for a special friend. Reminiscent of the old German feather trees, it's sure to bring old-world charm to any room. The border, quilted with pearl cotton, adds an extra dimension to the quilting. Finished quilt size, 33 × 33"; finished runner size, 17 × 40"; finished block size 11 × 11". Ornament size: 4 × 4".

Materials for Both Projects

- ½ yard green print fabric
- ¾ yard red print fabric
- 2½ yards tan or light brown fabric
- All-purpose threads to match fabrics and binding
- 35 × 35" piece of quilt batting (for the quilt)
- 35 × 35" piece of fabric (for the quilt backing)
- 19 × 42" piece of quilt batting (for the runner)
- 19 × 42" piece of fabric (for the runner backing)
- 1 skein of green pearl cotton
- 7 yards of tan or light brown double-fold quilt binding (folded width ½"; unfolded width, 2"): 4 yards for the quilt; 3 yards for the runner

Directions

Construction is done with right sides of fabric facing and seam allowances of ¼", which are included in the given measurements. Always press the seam allowances towards the darker fabrics. Identical blocks (figure 14–1) are made for the quilt and the runner; you need 4 blocks for the quilt and 2 for the runner. Cutting guides and directions give cutting and piecing for quilt and runner blocks together; the assembly of each project is given separately.

Making the Quilt and Runner Blocks

1. Following the cutting guides, cut all the strips necessary and tag them with the unit for which they will be used, so you can find them easily. The blocks are assembled from separate units (see figure 4–1), which we'll make next.

2. Take the tan 4½ × 22" strip and the green 1½" × 22" strip. Stitch them together along one long edge. Press the strip open. Using a ruler and rotary cutter (or a scissors), cut across both strips to make twelve 1½"-wide A units, as shown in figure 4–2. Set them aside.

3. To make the B units, take the 3½ × 22" tan strip and the green 2½ × 22" strip and stitch them together along one long side. Press open. Cut across

Green fabric cutting guide

Quantity and Size		Use
One	1½ × 22"	A units
One	2½ × 22"	B units
One	3½ × 22"	C units
One	4½ × 22"	D units
One	5½ × 22"	E units
Six	1½ × 10½"	trunks

Tan fabric cutting guide

Quantity and Size		Use
One	4½ × 22"	A units
One	3½ × 22"	B units
One	2½ × 22"	C units
One	1½ × 22"	D units
Three	5½ × 44"	F strips
Six	1½ × 11½"	G strips
Three	1½ × 25½"	H strips
Two	2½ × 27½"	middle borders, quilt
Two	2½ × 31½"	middle borders, quilt
Four	1½ × 11½"	I side bars, runner
Two	1½ × 13½"	Q strips, runner
One	12½ × 13½"	K block for runner

Red print fabric cutting guide

Quantity and Size		Use
Six	1½" × 1½"	treetop strips
Two	1½ × 25½"	inner border, quilt
Two	1½ × 27½"	inner border, quilt
Two	1½ × 33½"	outer border, quilt
Two	1½ × 31½"	outer border, quilt
Two	2½ × 36½"	L runner border
Two	2½ × 17½"	M runner border

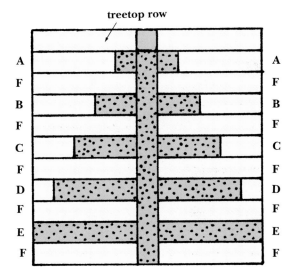

4–1: Block diagram for quilt and runner blocks.

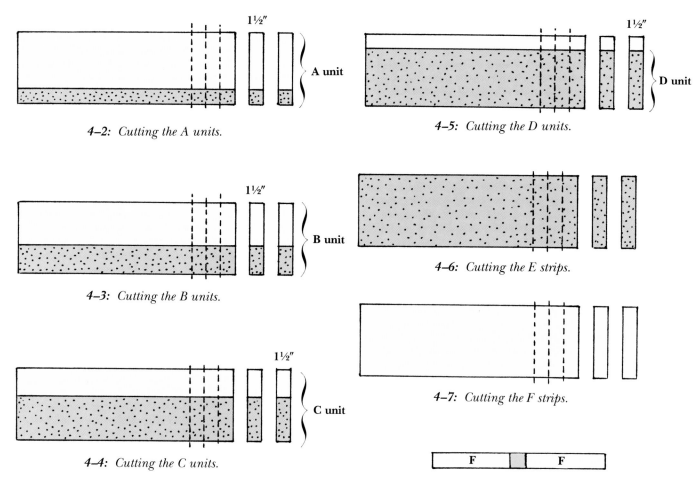

4–2: *Cutting the A units.*

4–3: *Cutting the B units.*

4–4: *Cutting the C units.*

4–5: *Cutting the D units.*

4–6: *Cutting the E strips.*

4–7: *Cutting the F strips.*

4–8: *The completed treetop row.*

both to make twelve 1½″-wide B units, as shown in figure 4–3. Set them aside.

4. To make the C units, take the tan 2½ × 22″ strip and the green 3½ × 22″ strip and stitch them together along one long edge; press the strip open. Cut across both strips to make twelve 1½″-wide C units, as shown in figure 4–4. Set them aside.

5. To make the D units, take the tan 1½ × 22″ strip and the green 4½ × 22″ strip and stitch them together along one long edge; press open. Cut across both strips to make twelve 1½″-wide D units, as shown in figure 4–5. Set them aside.

6. To make the E strips, take the green 5½ × 22″ strip and slice off twelve 1½″-wide E pieces, as shown in figure 4–6. Set them aside.

7. To make the 72 F strips, take the three tan 5½ × 44″ strips and cut off 72 1½″-wide pieces (see figure 4–7). Forty-eight F strips are for the quilt; 24 are for the runner. Set them aside.

8. Take a red 1½″ square. Stitch one F strip to each of two opposite sides of the red square as shown in figure 4–8. Press. This is a treetop row. Make 5 more treetop rows the same way. Set them aside.

9. To make the left side of one tree block, assemble units A, B, C, D, and E, alternating with 5 F strips, as

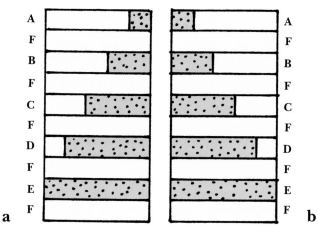

4–9: *Sides of the tree.* **a:** *The left side.* **b:** *The right side.*

shown in figure 4–9a. Press. Make the right side of the tree block as shown in figure 4–9b. It uses the same units as the left side, but they are assembled in a mirror image to the left side. Press. Make a total of 6 left sides and 6 right sides of the tree blocks in the same way.

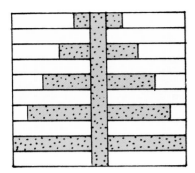

4–10: *The tree block without the top row.*

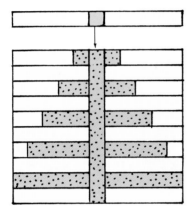

4–11: *Stitch the treetop row to the top of the tree.*

10. Take a green 1½ × 10½″ strip for the tree trunk. Stitch one left side and one right side of a tree to the trunk, as shown in figure 4–10. Make a total of 6 trees the same way. Press.

11. Stitch one of the treetop strips made in step 8 to the top of a tree block, as shown in figure 4–11 to complete the tree block; do the same for the other 5 tree blocks. Press the blocks.

Quilt Assembly (4-Block Quilt)

12. Take six tan 1½ × 11½″ G strips and three tan 1½ × 25½″ H strips. Stitch together 3 G strips, alternating with 2 tree blocks, to make a row as shown in figure 4–12a. Make a second row the same way. Press. Stitch the two tree rows to either side of an H strip and add two more H strips on the outer sides, as shown in figure 4–12b. Press. This makes the quilt center (figure 4–13).

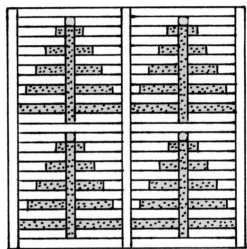

4–13: *Assembly diagram for the quilt center.*

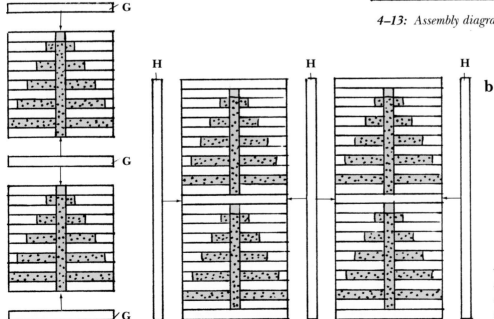

4–12. a: *Attaching the G strips to make a row for the quilt.* **b:** *Joining the parts of the quilt center.*

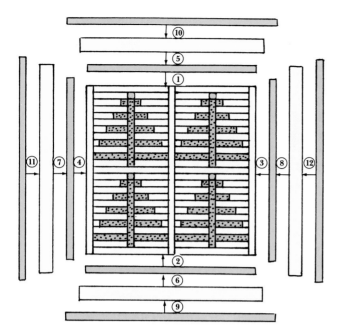

4–14: The border assembly diagram for the quilt. Numbers show order of piecing.

Border Attachment of Quilt and Finishing (4-Block Quilt)

13. Refer to figure 4–14 for steps 13 through 15. Take the two red 1½ × 25½″ strips and stitch one to the top edge and one to the bottom edge of the quilt center. Press. Take two 1½ × 27½″ red strips and stitch these to the sides. Press.

14. For the middle border, take the two tan 2½ × 27½″ strips and stitch one strip to the top edge of the quilt center and one to the bottom edge. Press. Take the two tan 2½ × 31½″ strips and stitch them to the side edges of the quilt. Press.

15. For the outer border, take the two red 1½ × 31½″ strips and stitch one to the top and one to the bottom edge of the quilt center. Take the two red 1½ × 33½″ strips and stitch them to the sides. Press. This completes the quilt-top assembly.

16. Using the border pattern, transfer the quilting lines to the tan border areas of the quilt top, referring to the photo as necessary.

17. Tape the 35 × 35″ piece of fabric, face down, to your work surface. Center the batting over it and center the quilt top, face up, over the batting. Hand-baste or pin-baste the layers together to prepare for quilting. Hand quilt or machine quilt the body of the quilt as desired (see the general directions).

18. To quilt the tan border, thread a large-eyed needle with a comfortable length of the green pearl cotton. Hand-quilt along the markings in the border.

19. Baste ¼″ in from the raw edges all around the quilt top. Trim away the excess batting and backing that extends beyond the edges of the quilt top to

prepare the quilt for the binding.

20. Bind the quilt with the bias binding.

Table Runner Assembly

21. For the table runner, take the four tan 1½ × 11½″ I strips for the side bars. Take two tan 1½ × 13½″ Q strips for the bottom bars of the blocks. Stitch the I strips to each side of one block. (Instructions for the blocks were given in steps 1 to 11 above.) Repeat for the second block. Stitch the Q strip to the bottom of each block, as shown in figure 4–15. Press.

22. Take the 12½ × 13½″ tan K block. Stitch one tree block to each 13½″ edge of the tan block so that the tops of the trees face the tan block (figure 4–16, center). This completes the runner center. Press.

23. Take the two red 2½ × 36½″ L border strips. Stitch one to each long side of the runner center (figure 4–16). Press. Take the two 2½ × 17½″ red M strips and stitch them to the two short ends of the runner. Press. This completes the runner top.

24. Transfer the pattern for the hand quilting, centered, onto the K block of the runner.

25. Tape the 19 × 42″ runner backing face down on your work surface, and center the batting over that; center the quilt top, face up, over that. Hand-baste or pin-baste the layers together and quilt the body of the runner as you wish.

26. Hand-quilt the central motif on the K square using the pearl cotton.

27. After quilting, baste about ¼″ in from the raw edges all around the quilt top. Trim away the batting and backing fabric that extend past the edges of the runner top.

28. Bind the runner with the bias binding to complete the project.

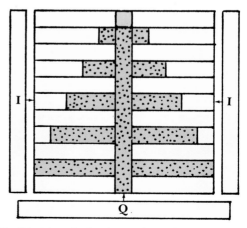

4–15: Stitching the I strips and the Q strips to the tree block for the runner.

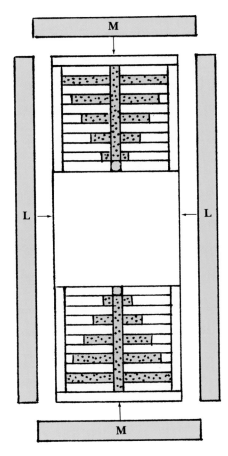

4–16: *Assembly of the runner.*

Materials to Make One Ornament

- 3½" square of tan fabric or another color
- 4" square of tear-away stabilizer or tracing paper
- Two 1 × 3½" strips red fabric (borders)
- Two 1 × 4½" strips red fabric (borders)
- 4½" square of red fabric for backing
- 4½" square of low-loft batting
- Green all-purpose thread for machine embroidery
- One small brown bead
- 5" length of ¼"-wide green satin ribbon

Make these ornaments in tan, or in your favorite colors to hang on your tree. You can pin them on the quilt or tack them in place with a few stitches. Finished size of ornament: 4 × 4", excluding hanging loop.

Directions

Construction is done with seam allowances of ¼" and right sides of fabric facing.

1. Trace the machine embroidery lines from the pattern (figure 4–17) onto the tan piece of fabric. Place the stabilizer against the wrong side of the marked tan square. Using the green thread and a medium-width machine satin stitch, embroider along the marked lines. Pull the thread tails to the back side of the piece and clip. Tear off the stabilizer and press the square.

2. Stitch the 3½"-long red border strips to the top and bottom of the embroidered tan square, as shown in figure 4–18. Stitch a 4½"-long red border strip to each side of the square to complete the ornament front. Press.

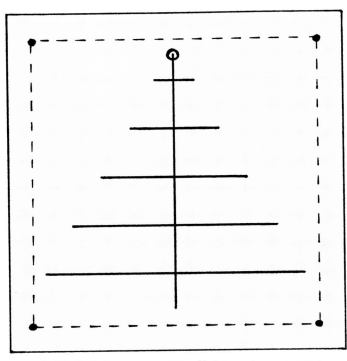

4–17: *Full-size pattern of the Christmas tree ornament, with embroidery lines (solid lines) and seam allowances (dashed lines). Small circle is bead placement.*

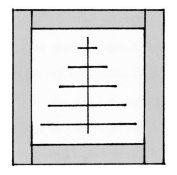

4–18: *Stitch the short borders and then the long borders to the center.*

3. Baste the 4½″ square of batting to the wrong side of the embroidered square, about ⅓″ in from the raw edges. Place the ornament front and the backing fabric square together, with right sides facing. Stitch along the side and bottom edges, and stitch along the top edge, leaving a 1″ opening along the top edge, as shown in figure 4–19. Clip the corners of the seam allowances and turn the ornament right-side out. Press.

4. Fold the length of ribbon in half to form a loop. Insert the ends of the loop into the center of the opening in the top of the ornament and hand-stitch the opening closed, encasing the ends of the loop in the stitching.

5. Hand-stitch the bead to the top of the tree as indicated by the small circle on the full-size pattern.

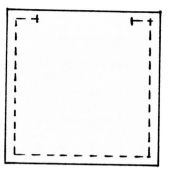

4–19: *Stitch the seam allowances, leaving a turning opening.*

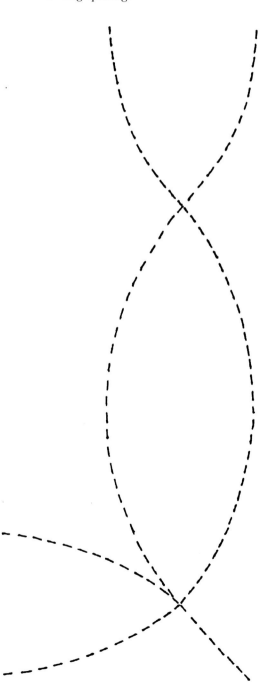

Full-size border quilting pattern for quilt

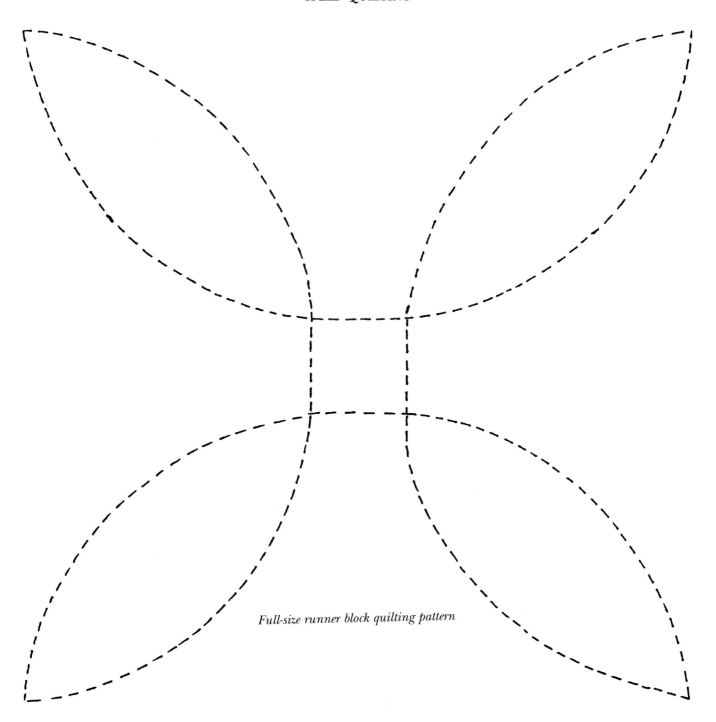

Full-size runner block quilting pattern

Hungry Mice Quilt and Placemat Set

Cute little mice have always been a favorite with children. Let these furry little critters scamper onto your walls and table with this set. And don't worry, they won't leave any "presents" behind! Finished size of wall quilt: 22 × 29″. Finished size of placemat: 13 × 16″. Block size: 10 × 7″. Finished size of napkin: 18 × 18″.

Materials for the Wall Quilt, Placemats, and Napkins*

- 1¼ yard tan print fabric for background areas
- ½ yard light gray fabric for mouse bodies
- ½ yard dark gray fabric for mouse bodies
- ½ yard deep rust fabric for sashing strips
- ½ yard green print fabric for the borders of quilt and placemat
- Seven 6 × 6″ scraps of five different yellow fabrics for the cheese (includes 2 for two napkins)
- 18 × 18″ piece of paper-backed fusible transfer webbing for the cheese (for machine appliqué)
- All-purpose sewing threads to match the fabrics
- Yellow hand-sewing thread if you will do hand appliqué
- 3 yards of rust double-fold quilt binding for the quilt (½″ folded width, 2″ unfolded width), plus 1¾ yards for each placemat
- 24 × 32″ piece of quilt batting for the quilt, plus 14 × 17″ piece of batting for *each* placemat
- 24 × 32″ piece of fabric for the quilt backing, plus 14 × 17″ piece of fabric for *each* placemat backing
- 3 small black buttons for the mouse eyes on the quilt, plus 1 for *each* placemat (or skein of black embroidery thread)

*Two placemat tops can be made from scraps of the quilt fabric. The tan yardage includes enough for two napkins. If you want napkins of other colors, you need a 19 × 19″ piece of fabric for each one.

Directions

Note: The quilt is made up of three mouse blocks plus a "cheese" row, separated by sashing. Each placemat also has a mouse block as its center. Construction is done with right sides of fabric facing and seam allowances of ¼″, which are included in the given measurements. The appliqué pattern (cheese) is given without

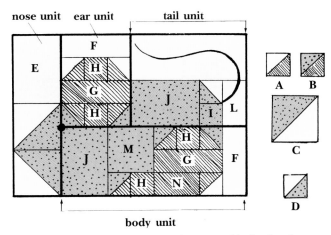

5-1: Construction diagram of a mouse block, showing ear, tail, nose, and body units (divided by thick lines).

seam allowances, which are not needed for machine appliqué (M steps); add ¼″ seam allowances around the pattern if you will do hand appliqué (H steps).

Making the Quilt

1. Cut and label all the strips and other pieces you will need for making the quilt, as listed in the cutting guides for each fabric.

Making the mouse blocks

2. Look at figure 5-1, the mouse block. It is made up of 4 large units, the nose, ear, tail, and body units. First we'll make some two-triangle squares by the speed method. For the *A squares:* Take the 7 × 5″ rectangle of dark gray fabric and one the same size of the tan fabric. Lay these pieces together, right sides facing. Mark six 1⅞″ squares on the wrong side of the gray fabric as shown in figure 5–2a. Mark diagonal lines through the squares as shown. Using a neutral-colored thread, stitch a line ¼″ away from EACH SIDE of the diagonal lines. Cut the squares apart along the marked lines. Then cut each square along the marked diagonal as shown in figure 5–2b. Press each unit open to make a tan–dark gray two-triangle

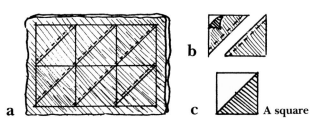

5-2: Making A squares. **a:** *Mark the squares and diagonals on the fabric and stitch on either side of the diagonal.* **b:** *Cut the squares apart, then cut along the diagonal lines. Press each unit open to form an A square.*

square; we'll call each an A square (figure 5–2c). (You will have 12 A squares, but will only need 9 for the quilt (3 for each mouse block). Discard the extras or save them for a placemat.) Set the A squares aside.

3. *B squares:* Take the two 9 × 5″ strips: one from the dark gray and one from the light gray fabric. Place the strips together, right sides facing, and mark eight 1⅞″ squares as shown in figure 5–3a. Make speed 2-triangle squares in the same way as you did for the A squares (figure 5–3b). Press each open to make 2-triangle light gray–dark gray B squares (figure 5–3c). You will have 16 B squares, but will only need 15 for the quilt (5 for each mouse block). Either discard the extra square or save it for a placemat. Set the B squares aside.

4. *C squares:* Take one 10 × 4″ strip of light gray fabric and one of tan fabric. Place the strips together, right sides facing, and mark three 2⅞″ squares on the wrong side of the tan fabric (figure 5–4a). Make speed 2-triangle squares as you did for the A and B squares (figure 5–4b). When you press them open, you will have 6 light gray–tan 2-triangle C squares (figure 5–4c). Set them aside.

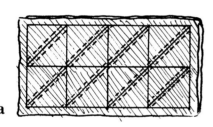

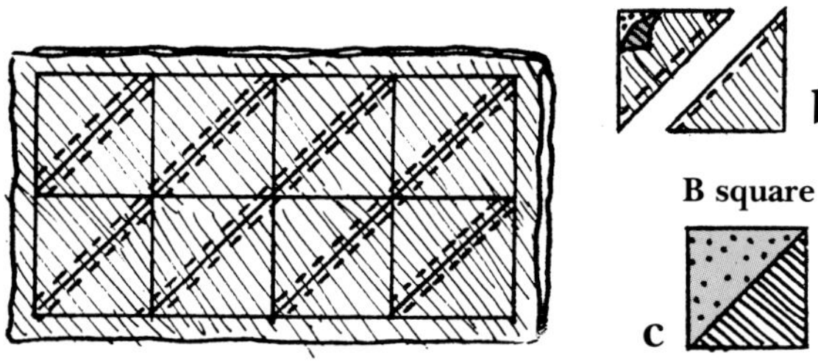

5-3: *Making B squares.* **a.** *Mark the squares and diagonals on the fabric and stitch on either side of the diagonal.* **b.** *Cut the squares apart, then cut along the diagonal lines.* **c.** *Press each unit open to form a B square.*

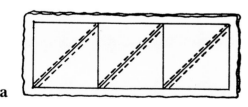

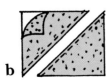

5-4: *Making C squares:* **a:** *Mark the squares and diagonals and stitch on either side of the diagonal.* **b.** *Cut the squares apart and cut along the diagonals.* **c:** *Press each unit open to form a C square.*

CUTTING GUIDES

Quantity and Size		*Use*

Tan print fabric cutting guide*

One	7 × 5″	A squares
One	10 × 4″	C squares
One	3 × 5″	D squares
Three	2½ × 3½″	E strip
Six	1½ × 3½″	F strip
Three	2½ × 5½″	K strip
Three	1½ × 2½″	L strip
One	5½ × 23½″	cheese strip

*If you are making tan napkins, cut a 19 × 19″ square for each, before you cut the smaller strips. You have enough fabric for 2 napkins included in your quilt yardage.

Dark gray fabric cutting guide

One	7 × 5″	A squares
One	9 × 5″	B squares
Six	1½ × 3½″	G strips
Twelve	1½ × 1½″	H squares
Three	1½ × 2½″	N strip

Light gray fabric cutting guide

One	9 × 5″	B squares
One	10 × 4″	C squares
One	3 × 5″	D squares
Three	1½ × 1½″	I squares
Six	2½ × 3½″	J strips
Three	2½ × 2½″	M squares

Deep rust fabric cutting guide

Four	1½ × 10½″	S sashing strip
Two	1½ × 5½″	T sashing strip
Three	1½ × 25½″	U sashing strip
for Each Placemat		
Two	1½ × 10½″	V inner border
Two	1½ × 9½″	W inner border

Green fabric cutting guide

Two	2½ × 25½″	side borders (quilt)
Two	2½ × 22½″	top/bottom border (quilt)
For Each Placemat		
Two	2½ × 12½″	X border
Two	2½ × 13½″	Y border

5. *D squares:* Take the 3 × 5″ strip of the light gray fabric and one of tan fabric. Place them right sides together and mark two 1⅞″ squares on the wrong side of the light gray fabric (figure 5–5a). Make speed two-triangle squares as you did for the A, B, and C squares. You will have 4 light gray–tan two-triangle D squares when you press them open (figure 5–4c). You will need 3 for the quilt (1 per mouse block). Set them aside.

6. Now we're ready to assemble a nose unit (see figure 5–6). Take a tan 2½ × 3½″ E strip and two C squares. Stitch them together as shown in figure 5–6. Make 2 more nose units the same way. Press them and set them aside.

7. Next we'll make the ear units. The ear unit is made up of four rows (see figure 5–7a). To make Row Two, join two A squares and a dark gray 1½″ H square as shown in figure 5–7b. Make 2 more of Row Two for the quilt and set them aside. To make Row Four of the ear unit, join two B squares with a dark gray 1½″ H square as shown in figure 5–7c. Make two more of Row Four the same way. To assemble an ear unit, take a tan F strip (1½ × 3½″) and a dark gray G strip (the same size). They are rows one and three of the ear

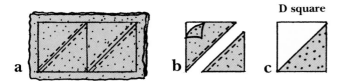

D square

5-5: *Making D squares:* **a:** *Mark the squares and diagonals and stitch on either side of the diagonal.* **b:** *Cut the squares apart and cut along the diagonals.* **c:** *Press each unit open to form a D square.*

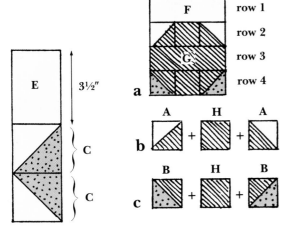

5-6: *The completed nose unit.*

5-7. a: *The completed ear unit.* **b:** *Making row 2 of the ear unit.* **c:** *Making row 4 of the ear unit.*

unit. Pin together the 4 rows of the ear unit, as shown in figure 5–7a, and stitch all 4 rows together to complete an ear unit. Make two more ear units for the quilt. Set them aside.

8. Next we can make the tail units; one is shown in figure 5–8a. First we'll assemble the bottom part, as shown in figure 5–8b. Take a D square, a 1½″ light gray I square, a light gray J strip (2½ × 3½″) and a tan L strip (1½ × 2½″). Stitch a D square to the I square as shown in figure 5-8b and stitch an L strip to its left. Stitch an L strip to the right to form the bottom of the tail unit. Add a tan K strip (2½ × 5½″ as shown in figure 5-8c to complete the tail unit. Make 2 more tail units the same way for the quilt. Draw the tail marking on each of these units as shown in figure 5–8a. Set the tail units aside.

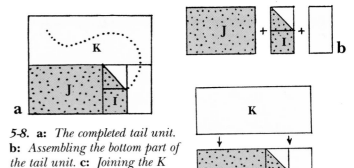

5-8. a: *The completed tail unit.* **b:** *Assembling the bottom part of the tail unit.* **c:** *Joining the K strip to the bottom of the tail unit.*

9. The body unit (figure 5–9a) consists of 2 pieced parts (Part 1 and Part 2) and an F strip. To make Part 1, refer to figure 5–9b. Stitch a B square to a dark gray H square (1½ × 1½″) as shown. Sew on a light gray M square (2½ × 2½″) and then a light gray J strip (2½ × 3½″) to complete Part 1. Make two more of Part 1 for the quilt (one for each mouse). Set the Part 1 units aside.

10. To make Part 2 of the body unit, refer to figure 5–9c. Make Row 1 of Part 2 by stitching together 2 B squares with a dark gray H square in between, as shown. Make two more of Row 1 and set them aside. Make Row 3 of Part 2 by stitching a dark gray N strip (2½ × 1½″) to an A square as shown. Make two more of Row 3 the same way. Row 2 of Part 2 is a dark gray G strip (1½ × 3½″). Assemble rows 1, 2, and 3 as shown in figure 5-9c and stitch them together to make a complete Part 2. Assemble two more of Part 2 the same way.

11. Now we can assemble the body unit. Referring to figure 5–9d, pin together Part 1, Part 2, and a tan F strip (1½ × 3½″) as shown in figure 5–9d, and stitch them together. Make two more body units the same way for the quilt.

12. Now we can assemble the nose unit, ear unit, tail

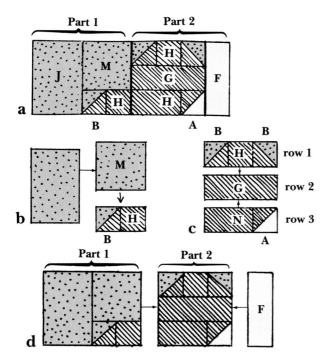

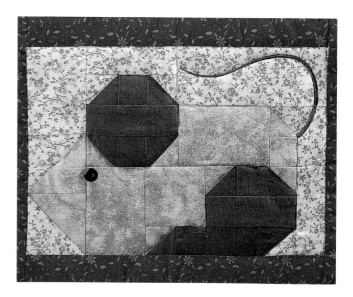

5-9. **a:** *The body unit, showing parts.* **b:** *Assembling Part 1 of the body unit.* **c:** *Assembling Part 2 of the body unit.* **d:** *Assembling the parts to make the body unit.*

unit, and body unit into a mouse block. Referring to 5–10, first stitch the ear unit to the tail unit, as shown. Next, stitch the body unit to the ear + tail unit as shown. Last, stitch a nose unit on. Assemble two more mouse blocks the same way for the quilt. Machine embroider the tails in satin stitch using the dark gray

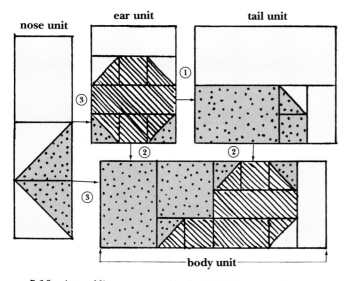

5-10: Assembling a mouse block. Stitch the ear unit to the tail unit. Then attach to the body unit. Stitch the nose unit on last.

thread, starting with the widest stitches at the body of the mouse and tapering the width of the satin stitch at the end of the tail. Set the mouse blocks aside.

Making the cheese strip

13M. To make the cheese strip of the quilt (figure 5–11, right) by *machine appliqué*, first trace 3 reversed cheese patterns onto the paper side of the fusible transfer webbing, and two unreversed cheese patterns; then cut out the cheese shapes roughly from the webbing and fuse them to the wrong side of 5 assorted yellow pieces of fabric with a warm iron. (See general instructions about fusible webbing, if necessary.) Cut out the shapes from the fabric; also trim away fabric in the holes in the cheese. Peel the paper off the fusible webbing. Place the 5 cheeses, evenly spaced, along the tan strip (see figure 5–11 for reference), keeping them one inch away from the top and bottom edges of the strip. Alternate reversed and unreversed cheeses as shown. Fuse them in place with a warm iron and machine appliqué them to the strip using matching threads and a medium-width machine satin stitch.

13H. *For hand appliqué,* trace the unreversed cheese pattern to the front of 3 pieces of yellow fabric and the reversed pattern to two pieces. Cut out the cheeses from the fabric, adding ³⁄₁₆″ seam allowances all around the pattern edges (including the inside of the holes). Pin or baste the cheeses in place evenly spaced on the tan strip as for machine appliqué, and hand appliqué them in place (see general directions for hand appliqué information).

Assembly and finishing of quilt

14. To assemble the quilt top, take the four deep rust 1½ × 10½″ (S) sashing strips. Referring to figure 5–11, stitch S sashing strips between the mouse blocks

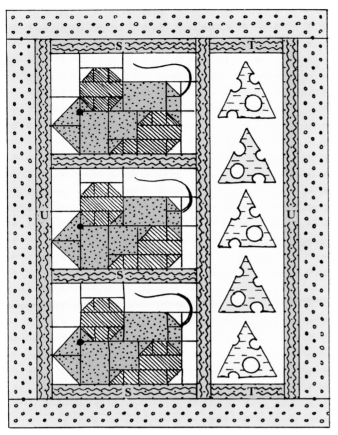

5-11: The construction diagram for the quilt.

and above the top mouse block and below the bottom mouse block. Press the seam allowances towards the rust strips. Set the mouse row aside.

15. Take the two 1½ × 5½" rust sashing strips (T). Stitch one of these strips to each short end of the cheese strip. Press the seam allowances towards the rust strips.

16. Take the three rust sashing strips that are 1½ × 25½" (U strips). Stitch one strip to each long side of the mouse block strip. Stitch the cheese strip to the U strip that is at the right of the mouse-block strip. Stitch the remaining rust U strip to the right long edge of the cheese strip. Press the seam allowances towards the rust strips.

17. To attach the borders, take the two green 2½ × 25½" border strips and stitch one to each of the two long sides of the quilt center, as seen in figure 5–11. Take the two green 2½ × 22½" border strips and stitch these to the top and bottom edges of the quilt top. Press the seam allowances towards the green strips.

18. Tape the quilt back, wrong side up, to your work surface. Center the batting over it and center the quilt top over the batting. Hand-baste or pin-baste the layers together. Hand quilt or machine quilt, as desired (see general directions).

19. After quilting, baste the layers together all around the quilt top, about ¼" in from the raw edges of the quilt top. Trim away any excess batting and backing that extend beyond the edges of the quilt top. Bind the quilt with the double-fold quilt binding.

20. Hand stitch a black button to the face of each mouse with gray thread. (If you are making the quilt for a small child or baby, embroider the eyes with 3-ply black embroidery thread instead.)

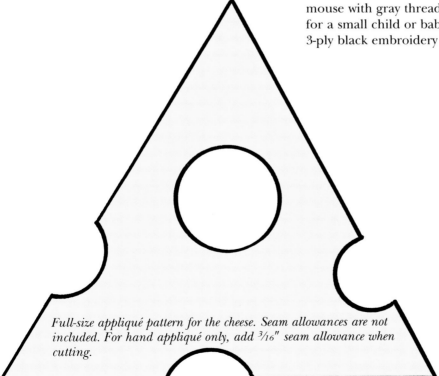

Full-size appliqué pattern for the cheese. Seam allowances are not included. For hand appliqué only, add ³⁄₁₆" seam allowance when cutting.

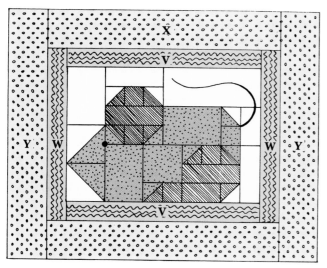

5-12: The construction diagram for the placemat.

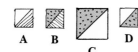

A   B   D
            C

Placemat

1. To make a placemat, make as many mouse blocks as you need (1 for each placemat), as explained in the directions for the quilt.
2. For each placemat, you need two 1½ × 10½" rust V strips and two 1½ × 9½" rust W strips. Stitch a V strip to the top of the mouse block as shown in figure 5-12 and one to the bottom of the placemat. Press. Stitch one 1½ × 9½" rust W strip to either side of the placemat.
3. Take the two green 2½" × 12½" X strips. Stitch

one to the top and one to the bottom of the placemat center. Take the two green 2½ × 13½" Y strips. Stitch one to either side of the placemat center. This completes the placemat top. Press.
4. Tape the placemat backing, face down, on your work surface, center the batting over it, and center the placemat top face up over that. Hand-baste or pin-baste the layers together. Quilt them as you wish.
5. After quilting, baste about ¼" in from the raw edges of the placemat top around all 4 sides and trim away any excess batting and backing that extends beyond the top. Bind the placemat with the binding and stitch the button in place for the eye.

Napkins

1. Double-hem the edges of a 19 × 19" square of fabric by turning under ¼" TWICE along each side and stitching the hem in place with matching thread.
2M. *To do machine appliqué,* for each napkin, trace one reversed cheese appliqué onto the paper side of the fusible transfer webbing. Cut the appliqué roughly out of the webbing and fuse the webbing piece to the wrong side of a yellow square of fabric. Carefully cut out the cheese shape, trimming away the inner circles of fabric in the holes as well. Fuse the cheese appliqué to one corner of the napkin. Machine appliqué the cheese in place with matching thread as you did for the quilt.
2H. *For hand appliqué,* trace the cheese appliqué to the front of the piece of yellow fabric, and cut it out, adding ³⁄₁₆" seam allowances as you go, on the inner curves of the holes as well. Pin or baste the appliqué in place and hand appliqué the cheese in place with matching thread.

Briar Rose Lap Quilt

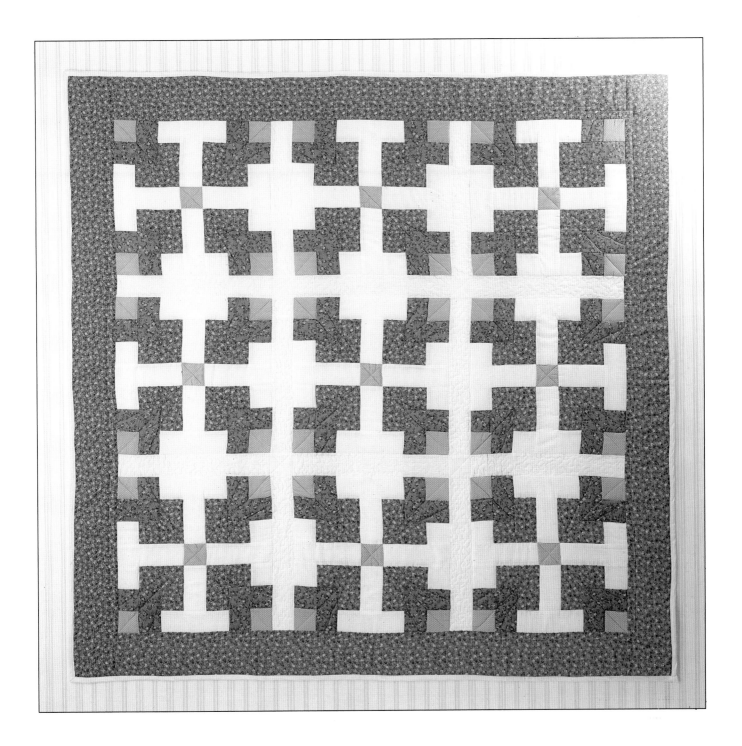

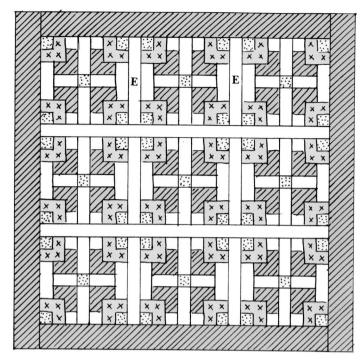

6–1: *Construction diagram of the quilt.*

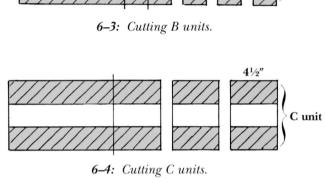

6–2: *Cutting A units.*

6–3: *Cutting B units.*

6–4: *Cutting C units.*

This is a very simple quilt to construct. It's based on a 2″ grid and has no bias edges or triangles. An average stitcher can easily have the quilt top made in less than a day. Finished quilt size: 54 × 54″. Finished block size: 14 × 14″.

Materials

- 1⅔ yards dark rose print fabric
- 1½ yards solid white fabric
- ¾ yard green print fabric
- ½ yard pink fabric
- 6¼ yards of white double-fold quilt binding (folded width, ½″; unfolded width, 2″)
- White all-purpose sewing thread
- 60 × 60″ piece of quilt batting
- 60 × 60″ piece of fabric for the backing

Directions

Construction is done with right sides of fabric facing and seam allowances of ¼″, which are included in all of the given measurements. The quilt center consists of 9 blocks, separated by sashing (see figure 6–1).

1. Referring to the cutting guides, cut the necessary strips of each fabric.

2. Take one pink, one green, and one white strip of size 2½ × 40″. Stitch them together on a long edge with the green in the center to make a 3-strip unit. Press all of the seam allowances in one direction. Make 2 more 3-strip units the same way. Referring to figure 6–2, cut across all three strips in the unit to make thirty-six 2½″-wide A units. (You will have some extra 3-strip units left over, which you can use to make an extra block for a pillow, if you wish.) Set the A units aside.

3. Take a green 4½ × 40″ strip and a rose 2½ × 40″ strip. Stitch the rose strip to the green strip along one long edge to make a 2-strip unit. Repeat to make two more 2-strip units. Cutting across the 2-strip units, cut a total of thirty-six 2½″-wide B units from the 2-strip units, as shown in figure 6–3. Set the B units aside.

4. Take the six 2½ × 40″ rose strips and 3 white strips the same size. Stitch a white strip between two rose strips on their long edges to make a 3-strip unit (see figure 6–4). Make another 3-strip unit the same way. Cutting across the 3-strip units, cut a total of eighteen 4½″-wide C units.

5. Now we can start assembling the blocks; see figure 6–5 for the block diagram. Referring to figure 6–6a, stitch one A unit and one B unit together as shown to make an AB unit. Repeat to make a total of 18 AB units. Set them aside.

CUTTING GUIDES

Quantity and Size		Use

Rose fabric cutting guide*

Nine	2½ × 40″	B units
Two	4½ × 46½″	borders
Two	4½ × 54½″	borders

*Cut all the dark rose strips on the *length* of the fabric (not across)

Green fabric cutting guide

Three	2½ × 40″	A units
Three	4½ × 40″	B units

Pink fabric cutting guide

Three	2½ × 40″	A unit
One	2½ × 25″	center block strip

White fabric cutting guide

Two	2½ × 46½″	sashing*
Nine	2½ × 40″	A units, C units, D strips
Two	6½ × 25″	center block strip
Six	2½ × 14″	sashing

*Cut the 46½″ sashing strips first, along the length of the fabric. Cut the rest across the width of the fabric.

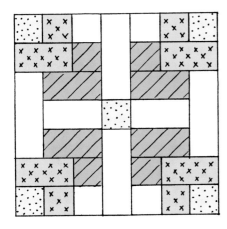

6–5: *Block diagram.*

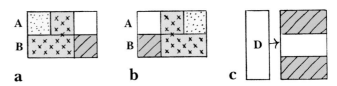

6–6: *Assembling units.* **a:** *The AB unit.* **b:** *The ABr unit.* **c:** *The D + C unit.*

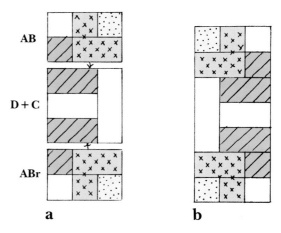

6–7: *Assembling a half of the quilt block.* **a:** *Assembling the left block unit.* **b:** *The completed left block unit. The right block unit is simply the left block unit, rotated 180°.*

6. Referring to 6–6b, stitch one A and one B unit together as shown to make a reversed AB unit (henceforth known as ABr). Make a total of 18 ABr units. Press all of the units. Set them aside.

7. Take three white 2½ × 40″ strips. From each of these strips cut six 2½ × 6½″ D strips, for a total of 18 D strips. Stitch one of these white strips to each of the 18 C units as shown in figure 6–6c to make a D + C unit. Press.

8. Now we can assemble the two halves of the block. Referring to figure 6–7a, make the left unit of the block by stitching together one AB, one ABr, and one D + C unit as shown (figure 6–7b shows the completed left unit). The right unit of the block is simply the left unit rotated 180° (that is, turned upside down), so make a total of 18 left units the same way. We will turn 9 of them upside down to be the right units of the blocks. Press. Set them aside.

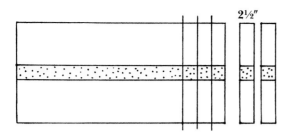

2½″

6–8: Cutting the center block strips.

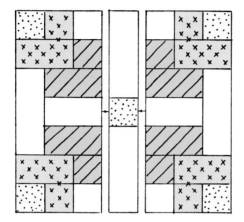

6–9: Stitching the block halves to the center block strip.

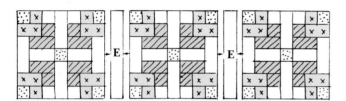

6–10: Stitching blocks and E strips to form a row.

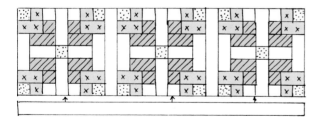

6–11: Stitching a long sashing strip to a block row.

9. Take the two white 6½ × 25″ strips and the pink 2½ × 25″ strip. Stitch one of the white strips to each long side of the pink strip. Press the seam allowances towards the pink strip. Cut across all three strips to make nine 2½″-wide pieces (figure 6–8). These are the center block strips.

10. Stitch one left block unit and one right block unit (a left unit rotated 180°) to the center strip as shown

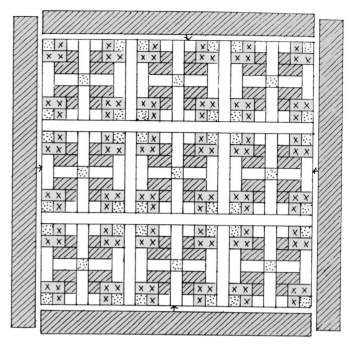

6–12: Stitching the borders to the quilt center.

in figure 6–9. Press. Make eight more blocks the same way.

11. Take the 6 white 2½ × 14½″ E sashing strips. Assemble a row of three blocks, stitching 2 E strips in between them as shown in figure 6–10. Make 2 more rows the same way. Press.

12. Assemble the quilt center by sewing a 2½ × 26″ long sashing strip to the bottom of 2 block rows as shown in figure 6–11, and then stitching the rows together as shown in the construction diagram (figure 6–1). The row without the long sashing strip is the bottom row of the quilt center. Press. This completes the quilt center.

13. Take the two rose 4½ × 46½″ border strips and stitch one to the top and one to the bottom of the quilt center. Press the seam allowances towards the rose strips. Take the rose 4½ × 54½″ border strips and stitch one to each of two opposite sides of the quilt center; press the seam allowances towards the rose fabric.

14. Tape the backing fabric, wrong side up, to your work surface. Center the batting over it, and center the quilt top, right side up, over the batting. Hand-baste or pin-baste the layers together and quilt it as you desire (see the general directions).

15. Baste through all three layers about ¼″ in from the raw edges of the quilt top. Trim away any excess batting and backing that extend beyond the edges of the quilt top.

16. Bind the quilt with the double-fold quilt binding to complete it.

Garden Lattice Lap Quilt

The center for this quilt can be made any size you choose, from wall-hanging to bed size. If you increase the center, you'll need to adjust the size of the borders and the amounts of fabric you buy also, of course. Whatever the size, choose a lively large-scale floral print from the home decorating fabric lines for the best results, or use a heavy cotton floral. Just make sure the flowers are BIG for maximum impact! Using prepackaged single-fold bias binding speeds up the production of this quilt, but you can also make your own bias binding very easily. Refer to the general directions for making bias tape. Finished size of the lap quilt: 40 × 46″.

Materials

- 28½ × 34½″ piece of a large-scale decorator print fabric
- 1 yard off-white solid fabric for the borders
- 9 yards of 1″-wide single-fold bias binding in off-white (equivalent to 3 packages of prepackaged bias binding)
- ½ yard of fusible fleece (18 × 45″) to pad the bias strips
- ¼ yard of colored print or solid fabric for the border flowers, in a color that matches the flowers in the decorator fabric (blue in the model)
- ¼ yard EACH of 3 different green fabrics for the leaves (total ¾ yard)
- 1 yard (18 × 36″) piece of paper-backed fusible transfer webbing
- 1 skein EACH of medium green and pink 6-strand embroidery floss
- All-purpose sewing threads to match the fabrics
- 45 × 50″ piece of traditional-weight quilt batting
- 45 × 50″ piece of fabric for the backing
- 5 yards of double-fold quilt binding in color of choice (green in the model; folded width ½″, unfolded width 2″)

Directions

Unless otherwise noted, construction is done with right sides of fabric facing and seam allowances of ¼″, which are included in all of the given measurements. The appliqué patterns are given without seam allowances, which are not needed for machine appliqué. For hand appliqué, add ³⁄₁₆″ seam allowances around the patterns before cutting. Steps for machine appliqué only are labeled M; for hand appliqué they are labeled H.

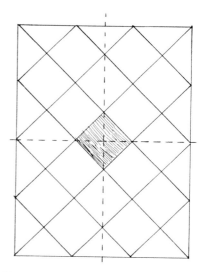

7–1: *Marking grid lines on the floral fabric. The 6″ center square (shaded) should be centered on the fold lines as shown as a first step.*

1. Fold the 28½ × 34½″ piece of floral fabric into quarters and press. Where the creases meet marks the center of the piece. Starting at the center of the fabric, draw the center guide square (shaded in figure 7–1), and mark grid lines, spacing them 6″ apart and drawing them at a 45-degree angle to the edges of the fabric, as shown in figure 7–1.

2. Cut a strip of the off-white bias binding as long as or ½″ longer than each of the grid lines you drew in step 1 (you can trim off any excess later). Cut a strip of fusible fleece that is slightly narrower than the bias binding across the width of your fleece. For instance, if your bias binding is exactly 1″ wide, cut the strip of fleece ⅞″ wide—you don't want any fleece extending beyond the edges of the tape. Trim a fleece strip to the correct length for each bias binding strip. Fuse the fleece strips to the wrong sides of the bias binding strips directly over the folded edges, as shown in figure 7–2. (Do not enclose the fleece in the seam allowances of the bias binding as it would add too much bulk.)

3. Lay the fleeced bias strips along the marked grid lines, centering the width of the bias strips over the marked lines (figure 7–3). Weave the strips over and under one another (see figure 7–6 for over–under pattern). Secure the bias strips for stitching with a water-soluble fabric glue stick or pins (the glue will hold the strips more securely, without any chance of the strips shifting while stitching).

4. Stitch the strips in place with matching thread or clear nylon monofilament and a machine blind stitch (figures 7–4a and b). The straight-stitch portion of the

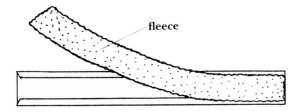

7–2: *A fleece strip is centered on the width of the wrong side of a bias strip.*

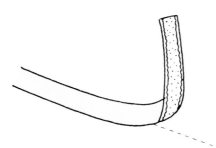

7–3: *Center each strip along a marked grid line.*

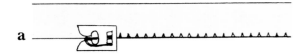

a

b

7–4: **a:** *Stitch the strips in place with blind-stitching.* **b:** *Detail of the blind stitch.*

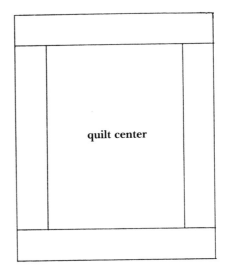

quilt center

7–5: *The borders, stitched to the quilt center.*

stitch should be on the floral fabric, and the zig-zag portion of the stitch should be on the bias strips. Stitch all of the strips in place to complete the quilt center. Trim off any lattice strip ends that extend beyond the quilt center.

5. From the off-white solid fabric, cut two 6½ × 34½" border strips and stitch one to each long side of the quilt center. Cut two 6½ × 40½" off-white border strips and stitch one to each of the remaining two sides of the quilt center. Press the seam allowances towards the quilt center (figure 7–5).

6M. *For machine appliqué,* trace 8 to 10 border blossoms and 24 to 26 leaves onto the paper side of the fusible transfer webbing. Roughly cut out the blossoms from the webbing and fuse the pieces with the traced blossoms to the wrong side of the colored fabric (blue in the model) with a warm iron. Roughly cut out and fuse ⅓ of the webbing leaves to the wrong

side of each of the green fabrics. Carefully cut out all of the appliqué shapes from their fabrics. Arrange the appliqué shapes on the borders around quilt top, keeping them at least 1¼" from the raw edges of the quilt top. When you have finished arranging them in a manner pleasing to you, peel off the paper on the webbing, pin or baste the appliqués in place, and fuse them to the borders with a warm iron. Machine appliqué each appliqué in place using a medium-width satin stitch and thread that matches the appliqué.

6H. *For hand appliqué,* trace 8 to 10 blossom shapes onto the front of the colored fabric (blue in the model), leaving enough room for 3⁄16" seam allowances on each piece, and cut them out of the fabric, adding the seam allowance as you cut. Trace a total of 24 to 26 leaves in the same way onto the front of the 3 green fabrics. Cut out all the appliqués from the fabrics and baste them in place on the borders. Appliqué each to the border with matching thread (see general directions for details of hand appliqué).

7. Draw the vines freehand with tailor's chalk or water-soluble pencil; don't worry, it's easier than you think! Draw a few curly tendrils here and there to fill in any areas that seem to need something extra (figure 7–6).

8. Separate about 18" of the green embroidery floss into two 3-strand lengths. Thread a needle with one of the three-strand lengths and embroider the vines by hand using the stem stitch (figure 7–7).

9. Embroider the tendrils in the same manner (figure 7–8).

10. Separate the pink floss into three strands as for the green floss. Embroider the flower centers by hand with french knots (figure 7–9a). Embroider a cluster

Full-size appliqué patterns, given without seam allowances. For hand-appliqué, add ³⁄₁₆″ seam allowances around the edges of the patterns as you cut them out.

of 8 to 10 french knots in the center of each flower (figure 7–9b).

11. Lay out the quilt backing, wrong side up, and center the batting and quilt top, right side up, over it. Hand-baste or pin-baste the layers together.

12. Hand quilt or machine quilt the project as desired, referring to the general directions if necessary.

13. After quilting, baste around all 4 sides of the quilt top about ¼″ in from the raw edges. Trim away the excess batting and backing that extend beyond the edges of the quilt top.

14. Bind the raw edges of the quilt with the double-fold green quilt binding to complete the quilt.

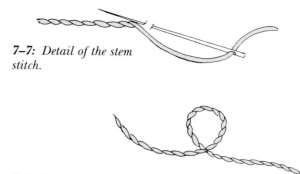

7–7: Detail of the stem stitch.

7–8: Detail of an embroidered tendril.

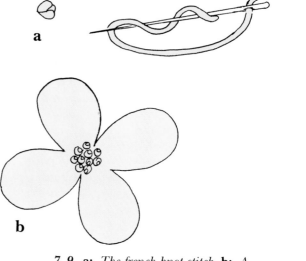

a

b

7–9. **a:** The french knot stitch. **b:** A cluster of french knots in the center of a flower.

7–6: Corner, showing freehand vines and tendrils in the border.

Potted Topiary Tree Quilts

A bright floral border and lilac ribbons set a romantic tone for these two projects. One of the green fabrics you choose should have just a hint of the same colors of flowers used in the border fabric. Block size: 5 × 13″. Finished size of the one-block quilt: 15 × 22″. Finished size of the three-block quilt: 28 × 22″.

Materials for Both Quilts

- ¼ yard of light green fabric
- ¼ yard of lilac fabric
- ¼ yard medium green fabric
- ½ yard of off-white solid fabric
- ½ yard of floral print fabric
- Two 12 × 15″ scraps: one of a light pink and one of a medium pink fabric
- 6 × 6″ scrap of light brown fabric for tree trunks
- 12 × 18″ piece of paper-backed fusible webbing for the bows
- All-purpose sewing threads to match the fabrics
- 17 × 26″ piece of quilt batting for one-block quilt
- 17 × 26″ piece of fabric for backing of one-block quilt
- 32 × 26″ piece of quilt batting for 3-block quilt
- 32 × 26″ piece of fabric for backing the 3-block quilt
- 5½ yards of green double-fold quilt binding (folded width, ½″; unfolded width, 2″): 2½ yards for the one-block quilt and 3 yards for the 3-block quilt

Directions

Construction is done with right sides of fabric facing and seam allowances of ¼″, which are included in all of the given measurements. The appliqué pattern (bow) is given without seam allowances, which are not needed for machine appliqué. Add ³⁄₁₆″ seam allowances around the appliqué patterns for hand appliqué. ("M" steps refer to machine appliqué only; "H" steps refer to hand appliqué only.) The block in the one-block quilt (figure 8–1) and the ones in the 3-block quilt are pieced in the same way. There is slight variation in the colors of some pieces in the outside trees of the 3-block quilt.

One-Block Quilt (figure 8–1)
1. See the cutting guides for the one block quilt and cut and label the strips and pieces. Next, we'll make some 2-triangle squares by the speed method.

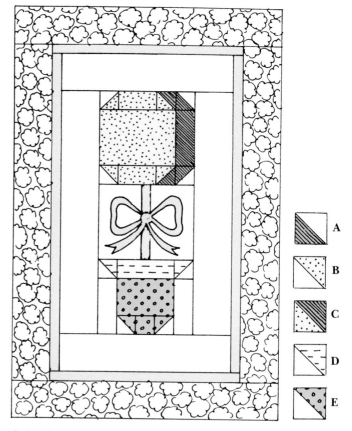

8–1: *Construction diagram of the one-block quilt (the tree block is the same as the center block of the three-block quilt).*

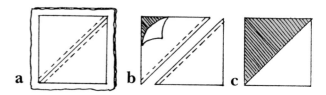

8–2: *Making A squares.* **a:** *Drawing lines and stitching.* **b:** *cutting the units apart.* **c:** *the finished A square.*

2. *A squares:* Take the medium green and the off-white 2½″ square. On the wrong side of one of these fabrics draw a 1⅞″ square. Draw a diagonal line through this square. Place the two squares of fabric together, right sides facing, and stitch ¼″ from each side of the diagonal line (figure 8–2a). Cut out the square along the marked lines, and cut it in half along the diagonal line (figure 8–2b). Press each resulting unit open to form a two-triangle off-white/medium green unit A square, as shown in figure 8–2c. Set them aside.

3. *B squares:* Repeat step 1 using an off-white and light green square of fabric, as shown in figure 8–3, to make the B squares. Set them aside.

One-Block Quilt Cutting Guides

Quantity and Size		Use
Off-white cutting guide: one-block quilt		
Four	2½ × 2½″	A, B, D, and E squares
Two	4½ × 2¾″	I strips
Two	1½ × 3½″	M strips
Two	2½ × 13½″	N strips
Two	2½ × 9½″	O strips
Light pink cutting guide: one-block quilt		
One	2½ × 2½″	for D squares
One	1½ × 3½″	J strip
Medium pink cutting guide: one-block quilt		
One	2½ × 2½″	E squares
One	3½ × 2½″	K strip
One	1½ × 1½″	L square
Light green cutting guide: one-block quilt		
Two	2½ × 2½″	for B and C squares
Two	2½ × 1½″	F strips
One	3½ × 4½″	G rectangle
Medium green cutting guide: one-block quilt		
Two	2½ × 2½″	for A and C squares
One	1½ × 3½″	H strip
Lilac cutting guide: one block quilt		
Two	1 × 17½″	border strips
Two	1 × 10½″	border strips
One	5 × 6″	for bow appliqué
Floral cutting guide: one-block quilt		
Two	2½ × 18½″	border strips
Two	2½ × 14½″	border strips
Light brown cutting guide: one-block quilt		
One	1 × 4½″	tree trunk

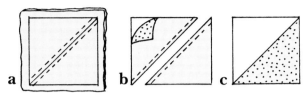

8–3: Making B squares. **a:** *Drawing lines and stitching.* **b:** *cutting the units apart.* **c:** *The finished B square.*

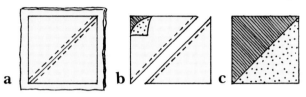

8–4: Making C squares. **a:** *Drawing lines and stitching.* **b:** *cutting the units apart.* **c:** *The finished C square.*

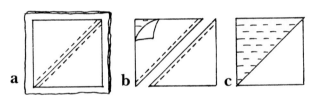

8–5: Making D squares. **a:** *Drawing lines and stitching.* **b:** *Cutting the units apart.* **c:** *The finished D square.*

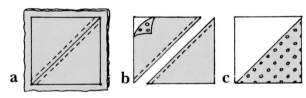

8–6: Making E squares. **a:** *Drawing lines and stitching.* **b:** *Cutting the units apart.* **c:** *The finished E square.*

4. *C squares:* Repeat step 1 using a light green and a medium green square, as shown in figure 8–4, to make the C squares. Set them aside.

5. *D squares:* Repeat step 1 using one light pink and one off-white square of fabric, as shown in figure 8–5, to make the D squares. Set them aside.

6. *E squares:* Repeat step 1 again, using one medium pink square and one off-white square of fabric, as shown in figure 8–6, to make the E squares. Set them aside.

7. Next we can assemble the three sections that make up the treetop. Referring to figure 8–7, assemble and stitch an A, B and C square along with a light green 1½ × 2½″ F strip to make the top section of the treetop. Take another A, B, and C square and an F strip and assemble and stitch the bottom unit, referring to figure 8–7, bottom. Press and set these two sections aside.

8. Take the medium green 1½ × 3½" H strip and stitch it to the light green 3½ × 4½" G rectangle to make the middle section of the treetop. Then assemble and stitch the top, middle and bottom treetop sections together as shown in figure 8–7. Press it and set it aside.

9. To make the center unit of the tree (figure 8–8), take the 1 × 4½" strip of light brown fabric and the two 4½ × 2¾" I strips of off white fabric (sounds strange, but it will work!). Stitch one of the off-white I strips to each side of the brown strip and press the seam allowances towards the brown fabric. You now have a tree center unit measuring 4½ × 5½".

10M. *For machine appliqué:* Trace the bow shape onto the paper side of the fusible webbing. Fuse the webbing bow to the wrong side of a scrap of the lilac fabric. Cut out the bow, remove the paper backing of the webbing, and fuse the bow in place on the center unit of the tree. Machine appliqué the bow in place using matching thread and a medium-width satin stitch (see general directions for machine appliqué).

10H. *For hand appliqué:* Trace the bow onto the right side of a scrap of the lilac fabric with a washable pen or pencil. Cut out the bow, adding ³⁄₁₆" seam allowances around the entire bow as you cut, as well as inside the loops. Prepare the bow for hand appliqué (see general directions for hand appliqué). Baste the bow in place on the center unit of the tree and hand appliqué it with lilac hand sewing thread.

11. To make the pot top, take the light pink fabric 1½ × 3½" J strip. Stitch one D square to each end of the pink J strip as shown in figure 8–9 to make a DJD unit; press it and set it aside.

12. To make the pot bottom, take the 3½ × 2½" medium pink K strip and a 1½" L square of the same fabric, plus 2 E squares. Stitch one E square to each of two opposite sides of the L square as shown in figure 8–10, and stitch the resulting ELE unit to one long edge of the medium pink K strip. Take two off-white fabric 1½ × 3½" M strips and stitch one of these to each side of the pot bottom (see figure 8–10). Press.

13. To assemble the block, first stitch the DJD unit made in step 10 to the pot bottom made in step 11. Then stitch the center unit of the tree above the pot, and stitch the treetop unit above the center unit (see figure 8–11). Press. This completes the block.

14. Take the two off-white 2½ × 13½" N strips and stitch one of these strips to each long side of the quilt block (see figure 8–1). Take two 2½ × 9½" O strips and stitch one to the top and one to the bottom of the block. Press. This makes the quilt center.

15. Take the two lilac 1 × 17½" strips and stitch one to each long side of the quilt center. Take two 1 × 10½" lilac strips and stitch them to the top and bottom of the quilt center. (These lilac strips will have

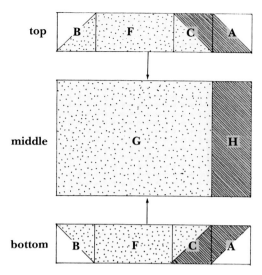

8–7: Assembling the treetop from its 3 parts (for one-block quilt and inner tree on 3-block quilt).

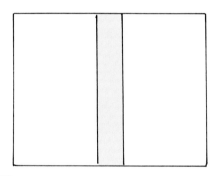

8–8: The center tree unit (bow is not appliquéd in place yet).

8–9: The pot top for the one-block quilt and the central block of the 3-block quilt.

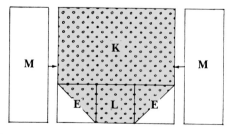

8–10: The pot bottom for the one-block quilt and the central block of the 3-block quilt.

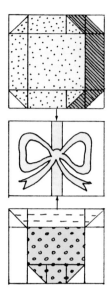

8–11: Assembling a tree block for the one-block quilt and the central block of the 3-block quilt.

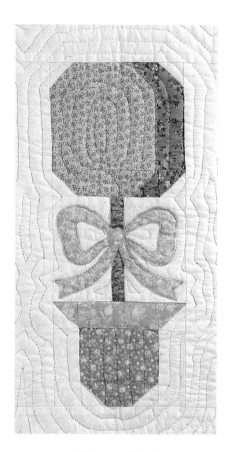

Closeup of block.

a finished width of only ½″, hence the 1″ cut width). Press.

16. Take the two floral print 2½ × 18½″ strips, and stitch one to each long side of the quilt center. Take the two 2½ × 14½″ floral print strips and stitch one to the top and one to the bottom of the quilt center. Press.

17. Lay out the backing fabric wrong-side up, center the batting over it, and center the quilt top right-side up over the batting. Hand-baste or pin-baste the layers together to secure them for quilting. Hand quilt or machine quilt the project, as desired.

18. Baste around the quilt top, about ¼″ in from the raw edge on all 4 sides. Trim away the excess batting and backing that extend beyond the edges of the quilt top.

19. Bind the quilt with the green binding to complete it.

Three-Block Quilt

See the cutting guides for the three-block quilt and cut and label the strips and pieces. Look at figure 8–12, the construction diagram for the three-block quilt. The center tree block is exactly like the one for the one-block quilt. The outer blocks have some pieces done in varying colors. The F and G pieces in the tree are medium green. The H pieces are light green. Also the colors in the pots are varied from the center block's. To make the 3-block quilt, we will need 6 each of the A, B, C, D, and E squares.

1. To make the A squares, take your 2½ × 6½″ pieces of fabric in the off-white and medium green, and trace out three 1⅞″ squares on the back of one piece. Draw a diagonal line through each square. Place the two rectangles of fabric together, right sides

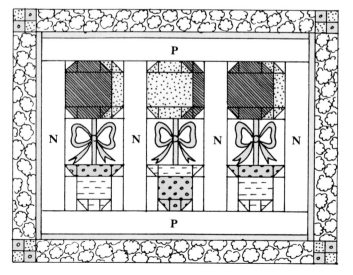

8–12: Construction diagram for the 3-block quilt.

Three-Block Quilt Cutting Guides

Quantity and Size		Use
Off-white cutting guide: three-block quilt		
Four	2½ × 6½″	A, B, D, and E squares
Six	4½ × 2¾″	I strips
Six	1½ × 3½″	M strips
Four	2½ × 13½″	N strips
Two	2½ × 23½″	P strips
Light pink cutting guide: three-block quilt		
One	2½ × 6½″	for D squares
One	1½ × 3½″	J strip
Two	3½ × 2½″	K strips
Two	1½ × 1½″	L squares
Medium pink cutting guide: three-block quilt		
One	2½ × 6½″	for E squares
One	3½ × 2½″	K strip
One	1½ × 1½″	L square
Two	1½ × 3½″	J strips
One	1½ × 14″	for corner units
Light green cutting guide: three-block quilt		
Two	2½ × 6½″	for B and C squares
Two	2½ × 1½″	F strips
One	3½ × 4½″	G rectangle
Two	1½ × 3½″	H strips
One	1½ × 14″	for corner units
Medium green cutting guide: three-block quilt		
Two	2½ × 6½″	for A and C squares
Two	1½ × 3½″	H strips
Two	3½ × 4½″	G strips
Lilac cutting guide: three-block quilt		
Two	1 × 23½″	border strips
Two	1 × 18½″	border strips
Three	5 × 6″	for bow appliqués
Floral cutting guide: three-block quilt		
Two	2½ × 18½″	border strips
Two	2½ × 24½″	border strips
Light brown cutting guide: three-block quilt		
Three	1 × 4½″	tree trunks

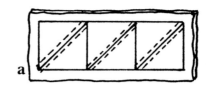

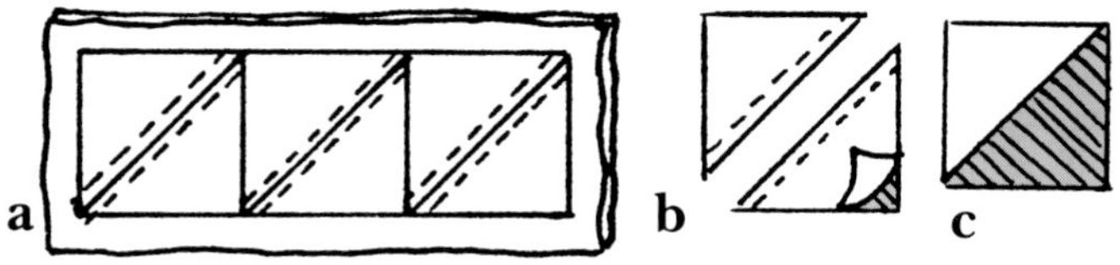

8–13: Cutting two-triangle squares. **a:** *Marking and stitching.* **b:** *Cutting the units apart.* **c:** *A finished 2-triangle square.*

facing, and stitch ¼″ from each side of the diagonal line (figure 8–13). Cut out the square along the marked lines, and cut it in half along the diagonal lines (figure 8–13b). Press each resulting unit open to form a two-triangle off-white/medium green unit A square, as shown in figure 8–13c. Set them aside.

2. Repeat step 1 with the 2½ × 6½″ off-white and light green fabric rectangles for the C squares; with off-white and light green fabric rectangles for the B squares; with off-white and light pink fabrics for the D squares; and with off-white and medium pink rectangles for the E squares. Set them aside.

3. Assemble the middle tree block as you did the block for the one-block quilt (see steps 7 through 12 of the one-block quilt instructions). Press and set it aside.

4. To assemble the two outside tree blocks of the three-block quilt, first we'll assemble the three sections that make up the treetop. Referring to figure 8–14, assemble and stitch an A, B and C unit along with a medium green 1½ × 2½″ F strip to make the top section of the treetop. Take another A, B, and C square and a medium green F strip and assemble and stitch the bottom unit, referring to figure 8–14, bottom. Press and set these two sections aside.

5. Take the light green 1½ × 3½″ H strip and stitch it to the medium green 3½ × 4½″ G rectangle to make the middle section of the treetop. Then assemble and stitch the top, middle and bottom treetop sections together as shown in figure 8–14. Make another treetop section the same way for the second outer tree. Press them and set them aside.

6. To make the center unit of the tree (figure 8–8), follow the instructions in Step 9 of the one-block tree quilt. Make two more center units the same way; press. Machine appliqué or hand appliqué their bows in place as you did for the one-block quilt (step 10). Set them aside.

7. To make pot tops for an outer block of the three-block quilt, take the medium pink fabric 1½ × 3½″ J strip. Stitch one E square to each short end as shown in figure 8–15, top, to make an EJE unit; make a second EJE unit the same way. Press them and set them aside.

8. To make the pot bottom for the outer block, take the 3½ × 2½" light pink K strip and a 1½" L square of the same fabric, plus 2 D squares. Stitch one D square to each of two opposite sides of the L square, as shown in figure 8–15, and stitch the resulting DLD unit to one long edge of the light pink K strip. Take two off-white fabric 1½ × 3½" M strips and stitch one of these to each side of the pot bottom (see figure 8–15). Make another pot bottom the same way. Press.

9. To assemble the outer tree blocks, first stitch the EJE unit made in step 7 to the pot bottom made in step 8. Repeat for the second outer block. Then stitch the center unit of the tree above the pot, and stitch the treetop unit above the center unit (see figure 8–16). Repeat for the second outer tree. Press. This completes the blocks.

10. Assemble the quilt center by alternating off-white 2½ × 13½" N strips with the three tree blocks, as shown in figure 8–12, and stitch them together. Press.

11. Take the two off-white 2½ × 23½" P strips. Stitch one to the top and one to the bottom of the quilt center (see figure 8–12 for reference). Press.

12. Take the two lilac 1" × 23½" strips and stitch one to the top and one to the bottom of the quilt center. Cut two 1" × 18½" lilac strips and stitch them to the short sides. Press.

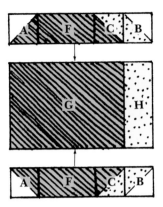

8–14: Assembling a treetop for the outer blocks of the 3-block quilt.

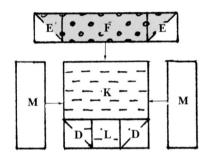

8–15: Assembling a pot for the outer blocks of the 3-block quilt.

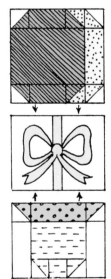

8–16: Assembling a tree block for the outer blocks of the 3-block quilt.

Full-size appliqué pattern for the bow, given without seam allowances. Add seam allowances of ³⁄₁₆" as you cut for hand appliqué only.

13. Take the medium pink a ½ × 14″ strip and the light green strip of the same size. Stitch them together on one long side. Cut eight 1½″-wide two-square pieces across both strips (figure 8–17a). Form the 4-patch corner units with 2 two-square pieces (figure 8–17b).

14. From the floral fabric, take two 2½ × 24½″ strips and stitch them to the top and bottom of the quilt center. Take two 2½ × 18½″ strips from the same fabric and stitch one of the 4-patch corner units made in step 13 to the short ends of both strips (figure 8–18). Stitch the resulting strips to the sides of the quilt top. Press. The completed quilt top will look like figure 8–12.

15. Lay out the quilt backing wrong side up, center the batting over it, and center the quilt top right side up over the batting. Baste, quilt, and bind the three-block quilt as you did for the one-block quilt.

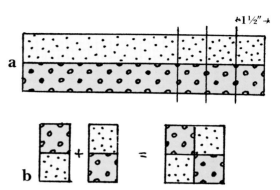

8–17: **a:** *Cutting strips for the 4-patch border corners.* **b:** *The finished corner.*

8–18: Two 4-patch corners attached to a short floral border strip.

Patchwork Angel Wall Hanging

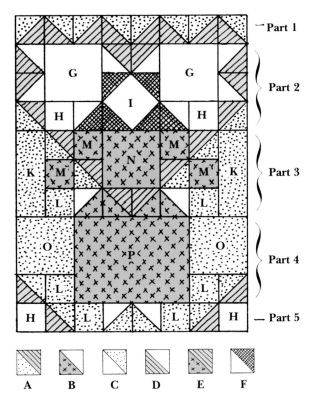

9–1: *Construction diagram for the Christmas Angel quilt center.*

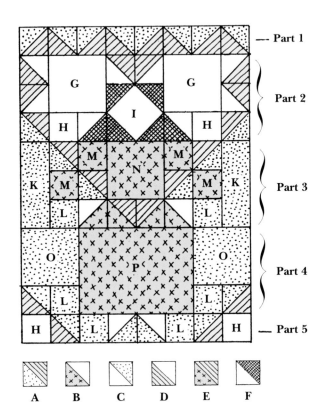

9–2: *Construction diagram for the Country Angel quilt center.*

Grace your walls this Christmas with a smiling patchwork Christmas angel. Stitched from bright Christmas prints, she's a lovely addition to your holiday decor, or stitch her country cousin from your favorite pastels and use her all year 'round. Finished size of each wall hanging: 24 × 30″.

Materials to Make Quilts

Christmas Angel Fabrics
- ½ yard green print
- ½ yard red print
- ½ yard white print
- ¼ yard off-white solid
- Scrap 5″ × 11″ flesh color
- Scrap 4 × 8″ deep gold print

Country Angel Fabrics
- ½ yard blue print
- ½ yard pink print
- ½ yard off-white print
- ¼ yard off-white solid
- Scrap 5 × 11″ flesh-color
- Scrap 4 × 8″ light brown print

For either quilt you ALSO need
- 2 small buttons for eyes (green for the Christmas quilt; blue for the country quilt) or black embroidery floss
- 26 × 32″ piece of quilt batting
- 26 × 32″ piece of fabric for the backing
- All-purpose sewing threads to match the fabrics
- 3¼ yards off-white double-fold quilt binding (folded width ½″; unfolded width, 2″)
- 1 skein EACH of brown, tan and red/pink 6-strand embroidery floss

Directions

Construction is done with right sides of fabric facing and seam allowances of ¼″, which are included in the given measurements. The following instructions are for the Christmas Angel (see figure 9–1). For the Country Angel, simply use the fabrics described in the Country Angel yardage requirements and cutting guides, substituting the pink where red is given in the Christmas Angel, etc. *To remind you, fabrics that need to be substituted for the Country Angel are given in brackets [ ] after the Christmas Angel fabrics in the directions.*

Green print (Christmas) or blue print (Country) cutting guide

Quantity and Size		Use
Two	2½ × 22″	border strips
Two	2½ × 20″	border strips
Four	2½″ × 2½″	M squares
One	4½ × 4½″	N square
Two	3½ × 3½″	for B and D squares
One	6½ × 8½″	P rectangle

Red print (Christmas) or pink print (Country) cutting guide

Quantity and Size		Use
Two	2½ × 26½″	border strips
Two	2½ × 20½″	border strips
One	7 × 17″	for A squares
One	3½ × 10½″	for D squares
One	3½″ × 3½″	for E squares

White print fabric (Christmas) or off-white print (Country) cutting guide

Quantity and Size		Use
Two	2½ × 6½″	K strips
Ten	2½ × 2½″	L squares
One	7 × 17″	for A squares
One	3½ × 3½″	for C squares
Two	4½ × 4½″	O squares

Off-white solid (Christmas or Country) cutting guide

Quantity and Size		Use
Two	4½ × 4½″	G squares
Four	2½ × 2½″	H squares
One	3½ × 10½″	for D squares
One	3½ × 3½″	for F squares

Flesh-colored fabric (Christmas or Country) cutting guide

Quantity and Size		Use
Three	3½ × 3½″	for B, C, and I squares

Deep gold print (Christmas) or light brown print (Country) cutting guide

Quantity and Size		Use
Two	2⅞ × 2⅞″ squares	for triangles
One	3½ × 3½″ square	for F squares

Country angel.

Cutting Pieces and Making the 2-Triangle Squares

1. The quilt is composed of squares, rectangles, and 2-triangle squares. The quilt will be assembled in 5 parts (see 9–1 or 9–2). First, cut out all the pieces listed in the cutting guides, using the correct color choices for whichever angel you are trying to make.

2. Next, we will make the two-triangle squares, using a speed method. Simply take the two fabric pieces as described in steps 3 to 8, and trace the number of 2⅞″ squares you are told to make onto the wrong side of one of the fabric pieces. Then draw a diagonal line through each square. Then, pin both pieces of fabric together with right sides facing and stitch ¼″ away from BOTH sides of the diagonal lines. If, for instance, the instructions call for two 8 × 8″ squares of fabric and you need to trace 4 squares onto the fabric, the stitched result will look something like figure 9–3a. After stitching, cut apart the squares along the marked square lines. Cut each square along the diagonal line also (see figure 9–3b). Press each resulting unit open to form a 2-triangle square (figure 9–3c).

3. To make the A squares, take a 7 × 17″ rectangle of red [pink]* print fabric and another of white print

---

*Bracketed colors are for the Country Angel.

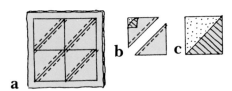

9–3: *Making two-triangle squares.* **a:** *Marking and stitching.* **b:** *Cutting.* **c:** *The finished unit (in this case, an A square).*

[off-white print] fabric. Referring to step 2, draw ten $2\frac{7}{8}'' \times 2\frac{7}{8}''$ squares on the wrong side of one of the pieces of fabric and draw diagonal lines through the squares. Pin the two pieces of fabric with right sides together and stitch along both sides of the diagonal lines, $\frac{1}{4}''$ away from the line. Cut apart the units and press each open to make an A square. You will have 20 A squares, but only need 18, so you may discard two of them. Set them aside.

4. From both the green print fabric and the flesh-colored fabric [blue print and flesh-colored fabric] take a $3\frac{1}{2}''$ square. Mark a $2\frac{7}{8}''$ square on the wrong side of one of the squares, mark its diagonal line, and stitch $\frac{1}{4}''$ away from the line along each side of the diagonal line. Cut the square on the ruled diagonal; press open the two halves to make two B squares, and set them aside.

5. From the white print fabric and the flesh-colored fabric [off-white print fabric and flesh-colored fabric], take two $3\frac{1}{2}''$ squares as you did in step #4, and stitch and cut two two-triangle squares; when pressed open each is a C square. Set them aside.

6. Take a piece of off-white solid fabric $3\frac{1}{2} \times 10\frac{1}{2}''$ [same for both angels] and one the same size of the red [pink] fabric. Mark 3 squares, add their diagonal lines, and stitch and cut $2\frac{7}{8}''$ two-triangle squares as you did in the previous steps. Press open the two-triangle units to make 6 D squares. Set them aside.

7. From the $3\frac{1}{2}''$ green print [blue print] square and the same sized red [pink] print square, make 2 E squares the same way you made the B squares in step 4. Press open the two E squares. Set them aside.

8. To make two F squares, stitch together a gold print [light brown print] and an off-white solid [same for both angels] $3\frac{1}{2}''$ square, as you did for the E squares. Cut them apart the same way, press open the two F squares, and set them aside.

9. Stack the squares in individual piles.

Assembling the Quilt Center Parts

See figures 9–1 or 9–2 for reference.

10. To make part 1 of the block, stitch eight A squares together as shown in figure 9–4. Press it and set it aside.

11. Part 2 has three sections, a left wing section, a

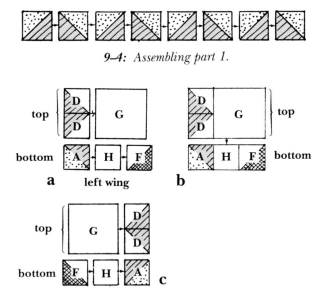

9–4: *Assembling part 1.*

9–5: *The wings.* **a:** *Making the left wing.* **b:** *Assembling the top and bottom of the left wing.* **c:** *Assembling the right wing.*

right wing section, and a head section. From the off-white solid fabric pieces [same for both angels] take two $4\frac{1}{2}''$ G squares and two $2\frac{1}{2}''$ H squares. Using four D squares, two A squares, and two F squares, plus the G and H squares, we will assemble one left wing section and one right wing section (see figure 9–8). For the bottom of the left wing, stitch an A square, an off-white H square, and an F square together as shown (9–5a, bottom). Set them aside. For the top of the left wing, stitch two D squares together and then stitch them to a G square as shown (9–5a, top). Last, join the left wing top and bottom (figure 9–5b). The right wing is made in the same order (see 9–5c). Set the wings aside after pressing them.

12. Take the flesh-colored $3\frac{1}{2}''$ I square [same for both angels] and two gold [light brown] $2\frac{7}{8}''$ squares. Cut each of the gold [light brown] squares in half on the diagonal to form two triangles for a total of 4 J triangles. Stitch one J triangle to each side of the I square to make the angel's head section, as shown in figure 9–6. Press it and set it aside.

13. Stitch two D squares together as shown in figure 9–7a and then stitch them to the head as shown (9–7b).

14. To assemble part 2 of the angel, stitch one wing section to each side of the head unit, as shown in figure 9–8.

15. Part 3 of the angel is made in three sections, as shown in figure 9–9. First we'll make the left section. From the white print fabric [off-white print fabric], take one $2\frac{1}{2} \times 6\frac{1}{2}''$ K strip and one $2\frac{1}{2}''$ L square. From the green print [blue print] fabric, take two $2\frac{1}{2}''$ M squares. Stitch together an A, M, and L square as

shown in figure 9–10a, and then attach a K strip as shown (9–10a). Add another row of an M, A, and a B square stitched as shown in figure 9–10b, to make the completed left side of part 3 (figure 9–10c). To make the right side of part 3, stitch together an M, A, and B square in a row, as shown in figure 9–11a. Then stitch

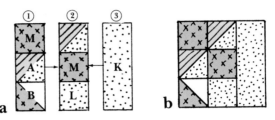

9–11: a: *Assembling the right side of part 3.* **b:** *The finished right side of part 3.*

9–6: *Assembling the head.*

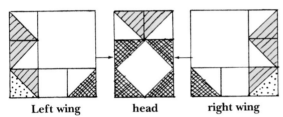

9–7: a: *Stitch the D squares together.* **b:** *Stitch the D squares to the head.*

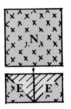

9–12: *Making the center of part 3.*

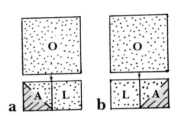

9–13: a: *The left side of part 4.* **b:** *The right side of part 4.*

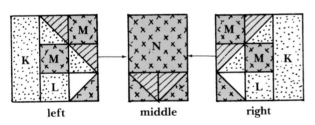

Left wing   head   right wing

9–8: *Assembling part 2.*

9–14: *Stitch one side unit to each short side of the P rectangle to form part 4.*

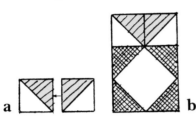

left   middle   right

9–9: *The components of part 3.*

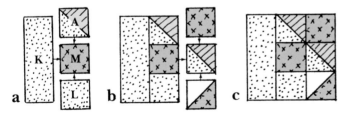

9–10: a *and* **b:** *Piecing the left side of part 3.* **c:** *The finished left side of part 3.*

an A, M, and L square together in a row. Join both rows to a K strip to make the completed right side of part 3 (figure 9–11b). Set it aside.

16. To make the middle of part 3, take the 4½″ green [blue] N square. Stitch two E squares together as shown in figure 9–12, and stitch this to an N square as shown. Press.

17. Stitch the left, middle, and right sides of part 3 together as shown in figure 9–9 and press. This completes part 3. Set it aside.

18. To make part 4, from the white print fabric [off-white print fabric] take two 4½″ O squares and two 2½″ L squares. Stitch one of each of these squares along with an A square as shown in figure 9–13a and b, to make a left side and a right side of part 4. Press.

19. To complete part 4, take the green [blue] 6½ × 8½″ P rectangle. Stitch the left and right sides of part 4 to the short sides of the green [blue] rectangle as shown in figure 9–14. Press it and set it aside.

20. To assemble part 5, take two off-white solid [the same for both angels] 2½″ H squares. From the white [off white] print fabric take two 2½″ L squares. Referring to figure 9–15, assemble these squares along with 2 A squares and 2 C squares, and stitch them together to make part 5, as shown. Press.

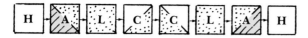

9-15: *Stitch the squares together to form part 5 of the quilt center.*

21. Stitch parts 1 through 5 together in order to form the quilt center (see figures 9–1 or 9–2 for reference) and press.

22. Referring to figure 9–16, take the two green [blue] 2½ × 22½″ borders and stitch these to the long sides of the quilt center. Press. Take the two green [blue] 2½ × 20½″ strips and stitch one to the top and one to the bottom of the quilt center. Press the seam allowances towards the green [blue] strips.

23. From the white print [off-white print] fabric, take four 2½″ L squares for the corner units. From the red [pink] fabric take the two 2½ × 26½″ outer border strips and stitch one of these to each long side of the quilt center. Take two red [pink] 2½ × 20½″ border strips; stitch one of the white print [off-white print] corner L squares to each short end of the two red [pink] strips. Stitch a strip that has the squares attached to the top of the quilt center and stitch one to the bottom of the quilt center (figure 9–16). Press.

24. Transfer the face markings (figure 9–17) to the angel's head (the I square) with water-soluble pencil.

25. Using 2 strands of the 6-strand floss in your needle, following the face markings, embroider the mouth in stem stitch with the red floss. Embroider the eye lashes with the brown floss. Embroider the nose with the tan floss. (If you want to embroider the eyes, instead of using buttons for eyes, do so at this point with black floss.) If the quilt is for a baby or a small child, use thread instead of buttons for eyes.

26. Tape the quilt backing, wrong side up, to your work surface, center the batting over it, and center the quilt top, right side up, over the batting. Hand baste or pin baste the layers together to prepare them for quilting. Hand quilt or machine quilt the project, as you wish.

27. Baste around all 4 sides of the quilt very close to the raw edges of the quilt top. Trim away the excess batting and backing that extends beyond the edges of the quilt top. Bind the quilt with the double-fold quilt binding.

28. Stitch the buttons to the eye area to complete the quilt, or use black embroidery thread to embroider the eyes.

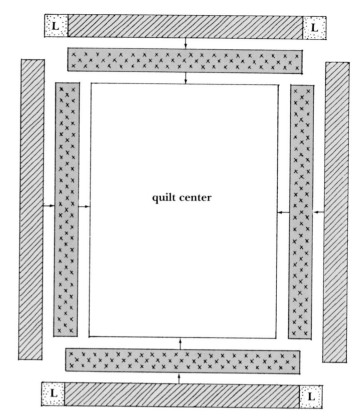

9-16: *Attaching the borders (Christmas Angel). For the Country Angel, the inner border is blue print; the outer border is pink print.*

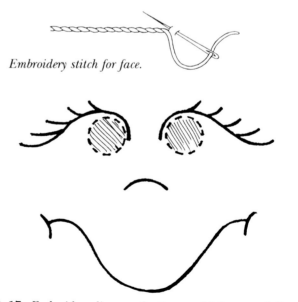

Embroidery stitch for face.

9-17: *Embroidery diagram for the angels' features, full-size.*

Fall Leaves Placemats and Napkins

A simple pieced leaf block forms the center of these quick-to-stitch placemats. Choose fabrics with a woodsy feel to give them character. This "recipe" makes two of each! Finished size of placemats: Approx. 16½ × 12½". Finished size of napkins: 18 × 18".

Materials for Two Place Settings

- 1 yard leaf print fabric with off-white background (includes enough for napkins)
- ¾ yard dark brown paisley print fabric (includes enough for backings)
- ½ yard rust print fabric
- ¼ yard of solid off-white fabric (or a second off-white print fabric)
- Two 18 × 14″ pieces of low-loft quilt batting
- All-purpose sewing threads to match the fabrics
- Safety pins for pin basting

Directions

Construction is done with right sides of fabric facing and seam allowances of ¼″, which are included in all of the given measurements.

1. Cut out all the pieces as indicated in the cutting guides.

2. Take the two off-white 19″ squares for the napkins. Hem each square along all 4 sides by turning under ¼″ twice along each edge and stitching the hem in place with matching thread. Set them aside.

Making 2-Triangle Squares and Assembling the Placemat Top

Next we'll make some 2-triangle squares for the placemats. They are all made in the same way, but some are smaller than others. See figure 10–1 for the construction diagram and list of 2-triangle squares.

3. We need to make 4 large rust–dark brown 2-triangle squares (2 per placemat), or A squares. Take a 4 × 8″ strip of both the rust fabric and the dark brown fabric. Draw two 2⅞″ squares on the wrong side of one of the fabrics and draw a diagonal line through each square as shown in figure 10–2a. Pin these strips together, right sides facing. Stitch ¼″ from each side of the diagonal lines (figure 10–2a). Cut the squares apart and then cut them in half along the diagonal line (figure 10–2b), forming 2 triangles from each square. Press each triangle open to make a 2½″ A square (10–1c). You will have 4 A squares. Set them aside.

4. Repeat step 3 using a 4 × 8″ strip of solid off-white fabric and a 4 × 8″ strip of rust fabric to make 4 B squares (you will have 2 extra squares). Set them aside.

5. Repeat step 3 again using a 4 × 8″ strip of solid off-white fabric and a 4 × 8″ strip of dark brown fabric to make 4 C squares (you will have 2 extra squares).

Off-white leaf print fabric cutting guide

Quantity and Size		Use
Two	19 × 19″	napkins*
Four	4½ × 4½″	for triangles
Four	1½ × 14½″	borders
Four	1½ × 12½″	borders

*Cut these first.

Rust fabric cutting guide

Quantity and Size		Use
Two	4 × 8″ strips	for A and C squares
Four	1½ × 8½″	border strips
Four	1½ × 10½″	border strips
One	3 × 6″ strip	for D squares
One	1½ × 17″	for side units

Dark brown fabric cutting guide

Quantity and Size		Use
Two	4 × 8″	for A and B squares
Two	2½ × 10½″	border strips
Two	18 × 14″	backings for placemats
One	1½ × 17″	for side units

Solid off-white fabric cutting guide

Quantity and Size		Use
Two	4 × 8″	for B and C squares
Two	3 × 6″	for D and E squares
Two	2½″ × 2½″	for stem blocks

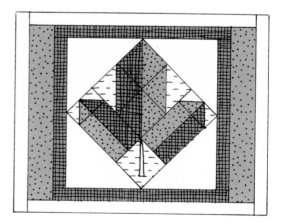

A B C D E

10–1: *Construction diagram of the placemat, with key showing 2-triangle squares. Finished size of A, B and C squares = 2″. Finished size of D and E squares = 1″.*

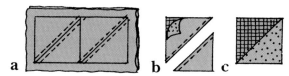

10–2: *Speed construction of two-triangle A squares.* **a:** *The marked fabric is placed over another rectangle of fabric and is stitched through both layers ¼″ away from the diagonal lines on both sides of the diagonal.* **b:** *The squares are cut apart and cut along the diagonals.* **c:** *The resulting two-triangle square is pressed open.*

6. We need to make some smaller 2-triangle squares also. Take a 3 × 6″ strip of the solid off-white fabric and one the same size of the rust fabric. Mark two 1⅞″ squares with diagonal lines on the wrong side of one strip. Stitch ¼″ from each diagonal line (figure 10–3a) and cut out squares, cut them in half on the diagonal lines (10–3b), and press open the 4 resulting D squares. Set them aside.

7. Repeat step 6 with a 3 × 6″ strip of solid off-white fabric and a strip of dark brown fabric the same size to make 4 E squares (figure 10–4). Set them aside.

8. Take the rust and dark brown 1½ × 17″ strips and stitch them together along one long edge; press the seam allowances to one side. Cut off four 3½″ wide pieces from the 2-strip unit, as shown in figure 10–5. These are for the side units of the leaf. You need 2 per placemat. Press and set them aside.

9. Take two 2½″ solid off-white fabric squares. To make the leaf stem, mark a diagonal line ¾ of the way up each square. Machine satin-stitch along this diagonal line, starting with a narrow width of stitch at the corner of the square, and widening it slightly towards the opposite end (figure 10–6). Do this on both 2½″ solid off-white squares.

10. To make the side points of the leaf, stitch together an E and a D 2-triangle square as shown in figure 10–7 to make a DE unit. Make 4 DE units (2 for each placemat), and press them.

11. To finish the leaf side, stitch a DE unit to a 2-strip unit made in step 8, as shown in figure 10–8a. Make three more leaf sides the same way. Stitch one of the leaf sides to one of the stem squares as shown in figure 10–8b. Repeat this with one more leaf side and stem square. Set the leaf sides aside.

12. To assemble the four 2-triangle squares for the top of the block, stitch a B square to an A square as shown in the top part of 10–9. Stitch another A square to a C square as shown in the bottom of figure 10–9. Then join the two rows of triangle squares to finish the top of the leaf block. Repeat to make a second leaf block top for the second placemat. Press them and set them aside.

13. Stitch together two leaf sides (one with a stem)

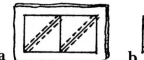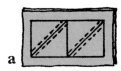

10–3: *Making the D squares.* **a:** *Marking and sewing.* **b:** *Cutting apart.* **c:** *The finished D square.*

10–4: *Making the E squares.* **a:** *Marking and sewing.* **b:** *Cutting apart.* **c:** *The finished E square.*

← 3½″ →

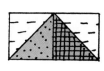

10–5: *Cutting the two-strip units.*

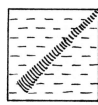

10–6: *Detail of the satin stitch used to embroider the stems by machine, showing change in stitch width.*

10–7: *An E and D square are stitched together in a DE unit for the point of the side of the leaf.*

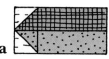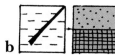

10–8: **a:** *The DE unit is stitched to a 2-strip unit to make the side of the leaf.* **b:** *The stem square is attached to a leaf side.*

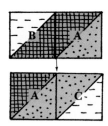

10–9: Making the leaf top. An A square and a B square are stitched together as shown (top row). An A square and a C square are stitched together as shown (bottom row). Then the two rows are joined.

and a leaf top as shown in figure 10–10 to complete the leaf. Make another leaf the same way and press them.

14. Take the four 4½″ squares of the off-white leaf print fabric. Cut each square in half on the diagonal to make 2 triangles. Stitch one of these triangles on its long side to each side of the leaf block (see figure 10–11). This completes the placemat center. Press.

Attaching the Borders

15. Take two 1½ × 8½″ rust strips. Stitch one of these strips to each of two opposite sides of the placemat center (figure 10–12). Do the same for the second placemat center. Press.

16. Take two 1½ × 10½″ rust strips. Stitch one of these to the top and one to the bottom of the placemat center, as shown in figure 10–12. Do the same for the second placemat center. Press.

17. Take two 2½ × 10½″ dark brown border strips and stitch one strip to each side of the placemat center, as shown in figure 10–12. Repeat for the second placemat. Press.

18. Take two 1½ × 14½″ off-white print strips and stitch one to the top and one to the bottom of the placemat center. Take two 1½ × 12½″ off-white print strips and stitch these to the sides of the placemat center. Repeat for the second placemat. This completes the placemat tops. Press.

Basting, Binding, and Quilting

19. Baste the batting to the wrong side of each placemat section. Baste about ¼″ in from the raw edges of the placemat tops and trim away the excess batting that extends beyond the edges of the placemat tops.

20. Pin one dark brown backing piece against one placemat front, with right sides together, and stitch around all 4 sides, leaving a 4″ opening along one edge for turning it right side out. Clip the corners of the seam allowances and turn the placemat right side

out. Hand-stitch the turning opening closed. Repeat with the second placemat. Press.

21. Pin-baste the layers of the placemat with small safety pins to keep them from shifting and hand quilt or machine quilt the placemats as desired.

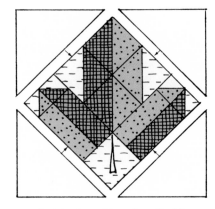

10–10: Assembling a leaf from two leaf sides and a leaf top.

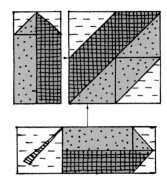

10–11: Attaching the off-white triangles.

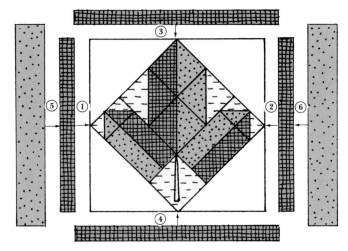

10–12: Attaching the rust and dark brown borders. Numbers indicate order of piecing.

Nine-Patch with Hearts Quilt and Tote

Lively floral fabrics in country colors make this quilt look complex, but it's actually a very simple project. Choose colors to match your decor. Finished quilt size: 28 × 28″. Finished tote size (excluding handles): 14 × 16″.

Materials for Both Projects

- 1 yard tan small-scale print fabric
- 1¼ yard large-scale blue and pink floral print fabric
- ¼ yard blue fabric (small print or solid)
- ⅓ yard pink fabric (small print or solid)
- 10″ square of paper-backed fusible webbing for the heart appliqués (needed for machine appliqué only)
- 30″ square of quilt batting (for the quilt)
- 30″ square of fabric of choice for the quilt backing
- 4 yards of double-fold quilt binding in blue (folded width, ½″; unfolded width, 2″)
- Two 15 × 17″ pieces of fleece or low-loft batting for the tote
- Two 1″ × 18″ strips of fleece or low-loft batting for the tote handles
- All-purpose threads to match the fabrics
- Tan hand-sewing thread (for hand appliqué only)

Directions

Construction is done with right sides of fabric facing and seam allowances of ¼″, which are included in all of the given measurements. The appliqué is given without seam allowances, which are not needed for machine appliqué (''M'' steps). If you will do hand appliqué (''H'' steps), add 3/16″ seam allowances around the hearts when you cut them.

1. Cut out all the fabric pieces for the quilt and tote, as shown in the cutting guides.

Nine-Patch Quilt

2. Look at the construction diagram (figure 11–1). You will see eight 9-patch blocks in the pieced border of the quilt. We will make them next, plus two extra blocks for the tote. Stitch one 1½ × 44″ blue strip to each side of one of the tan 1½ × 44″ strips, as shown in figure 11–2. Press. For the quilt, cut sixteen 1½″-wide A units from the 3-strip blue-tan-blue unit. Cut an additional 4 A units for the tote's 9-patch blocks. Set them all aside.

3. Stitch one 1½ × 44″ tan strip to each side of the pink 1½ × 44″ strip as shown in figure 11–3. For the

11–1: *Construction diagram for quilt top, with color key.*

blue   floral   tan print   pink

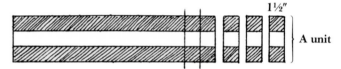

11–2: *Stitch three strips as shown and cut A units.*

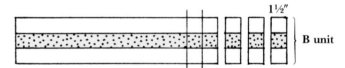

11–3: *Stitch three strips as shown and cut B units.*

quilt, cut eight 1½″-wide B units from the 3-strip tan-pink-tan unit; cut two more B units for the tote.

4. Stitch one A unit to the left side and one to the right side of a B unit, as shown in figure 11–4, to make a 9-patch block. Press. Make the rest of the 9-patch blocks the same way. You will need 10 nine-patch blocks (8 for the quilt and 2 for the tote).

5. Refer to figure 11–5 and stitch one tan 1½ × 3½″ spacer strip to each of two opposite sides of a nine-patch block. Stitch one 3½ × 4½″ floral print rectangle to the other two sides of each spacer to make a short pieced border (see 11–5). Make a second short pieced border the same way. Press them.

6. Stitch a tan 1½ × 13½″ sashing strip to each of

Cutting Guides (Both Projects)

Quantity and Size		Use

Tan print fabric cutting guide

Three	1½ × 44″ strips	9-patch blocks
Ten	1½ × 3½″ strips	quilt spacers
Four	1½ × 13½″ strips	quilt sashing
Four	1½ × 23½″ strips	quilt sashing
Four	5 × 5″ scraps	for appliqués
Two	2 × 25½″	quilt border
Two	2 × 28½″	quilt border
Four	1½ × 3½″	spacers for tote
Two	1½ × 14½″	strips for tote

Large floral print cutting guide*

Eight	3½ × 4½″	pieced quilt border
One	11½ × 11½″*	center quilt block
One	3½ × 4½″	pieced tote border
One	2½ × 14½″	for tote
One	7½ × 14½″*	for tote
Three	14½ × 16½″*	tote backing and lining
Two	3½ × 18½″	tote handles

*Cut the large pieces first.

Blue fabric cutting guide

Two	1½ × 44″	9-patch blocks

Pink fabric cutting guide

One	1½ × 44″	9-patch blocks
Two	1½ × 11½″	border of central quilt block
Two	1½ × 13½″	border of central quilt block
Two	1½ × 23½″	inner border of quilt
Two	1½ × 14½″	inner border of quilt
Two	1½ × 14½″	tote front

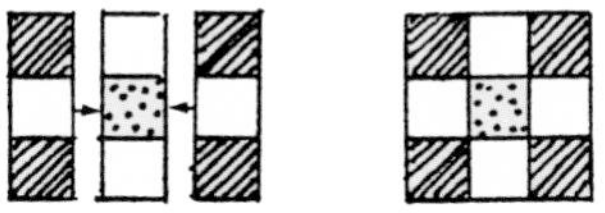

11–4: Make a 9-patch block from 2 A units and one B unit.
a: *Stitching the 3 units.* **b:** *The finished 9-patch block.*

the long sides of each short pieced border (figure 11–5). Repeat for the second short pieced border. Set them aside.

7. Make a long pieced border row from three 9-patch units, 6 short (1½ × 3½″) spacer strips, and 2

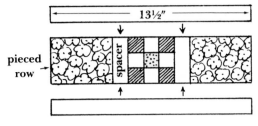

11–5: Stitch two 13½″ tan strips to a pieced row to make a short pieced border row.

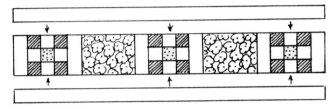

11–6: Stitch two 23½″ tan strips to a long pieced row to make a long pieced border row.

floral print rectangles (3½ × 4½″), as shown in figure 11–6, center. Stitch one of the 1½ × 23½″ tan sashing strips along each long edge of the long pieced border row (see 11–6). Make a second long pieced border row the same way. Press them and set them aside.

8M. *For machine appliqué,* take the 11½″ floral print square. Fold it in half on the diagonal and then in quarters on the other diagonal. Press the lines to serve as guidelines for positioning the appliqués. Set it aside. Trace 4 hearts onto the paper side of the piece of fusible webbing, cut them out of the webbing, and fuse each webbing heart to the wrong side of a 5 × 5″ scrap of tan fabric. Carefully cut the hearts out of the fabric. Remove the paper from the webbing, and position the hearts symmetrically on the fold lines of the front of the floral square (see 11–7). Fuse the hearts in place with a warm iron. Machine appliqué the hearts in place using blue all-purpose thread and satin stitch. See general directions for more information on machine appliqué, if necessary.

8H. *For hand appliqué:* Take the 11½″ floral print square and fold it in half and in quarters on the diagonals and press it to make guidelines for positioning the appliqués. Set it aside. Trace out 4 heart appliqué patterns onto the right sides of the four 5 × 5″ pieces of tan print fabric with a washable pencil or chalk, leaving enough room around each for seam allowances. Cut out the 4 hearts, adding ³⁄₁₆″ seam allowance around each one as you cut. Pin or baste the hearts in position on the diagonal lines of the 11½″ floral print square (see 11–7 for reference). Hand appliqué the hearts in place. See general directions for more hand appliqué instructions, if necessary.

9. Take the two 1½ × 11½″ pink strips and stitch

one to each of two opposite sides of the appliquéd floral square (see figure 11–7). Then take the two pink 1½ × 13½″ strips and stitch them to the remaining two sides of the floral square to make the quilt center. Press.

10. Stitch one of the 13½″ pieced border rows made in step 6 to each of two opposite sides of the quilt center, as shown in figure 11–8. Press. Stitch one of the long (23½″) pieced border rows made in step 7 to the top and one to the bottom of the quilt center (figure 11–8). Press.

11. Refer to figure 11–9 for stitching on the pink and tan borders. Take the two pink 1½ × 23½″ strips and stitch one to each of two opposite sides of the quilt center. Take the two 1½ × 25½″ pink strips and stitch them to the remaining two sides of the quilt center. Press.

12. Stitch one of the 2 × 25½″ tan strips to the top of the quilt center and one to the bottom of the quilt center. Stitch one of the 2 × 28½″ tan strips to each of the remaining two sides of the quilt center. This completes the quilt top. Press. The finished quilt top will look like figure 11–1.

13. Tape the 30 × 30″ piece of quilt backing to your work surface, right side down. Center the batting over the backing, and center the quilt top, face up, over the batting. Hand baste or pin baste the layers together and machine quilt it as you wish.

14. Baste close to the raw edges of the quilt top all around the quilt, and trim away the excess batting and backing fabric that extend beyond the quilt top. Bind the quilt with blue bias binding.

Tote Bag

1. To make the tote bag, take the 2 extra nine-patch blocks you made when you made the quilt blocks, or make two if you haven't done so yet. Take a 3½ × 4½″ floral print rectangle and four 1½ × 3½″ short tan spacers. Stitch the nine-patch units along with the floral print rectangle and the spacers to make a pieced row as shown in figure 11–10.

2. Take a 1½″ × 14½″ pink strip and a tan strip the same length, and seam them together on one long side. Make a second tan-pink 2-strip unit the same way. Then stitch one of the 2-strip units to the top of the pieced row you made in step 1 and one to the bottom (see figure 11–11). Press.

3. Take the 2½ × 14½″ floral print strip and sew it to the bottom of the unit you made in step 2, as shown in figure 11–12. Sew the 7½ × 14½″ floral print strip to the top (see figure 11–12). Press. This makes the bag front.

4. Baste a 15 × 17″ piece of fleece or low-loft batting to the wrong side of the bag front and baste the second 15 × 17″ piece of fleece to the wrong side of one of the 14½ × 16½″ pieces of floral print

foldline

11–7: The center floral block of the quilt, showing appliqué positioning. Dashed lines are fold lines.

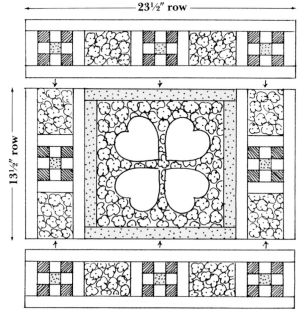

11–8: Attaching the long pieced border rows to the appliqué block.

fabric, which will become the back of the bag. Set it aside. Quilt the tote front as you wish at this point. You may need to put some stabilizer under the batting so the tote front can feed evenly in your sewing machine and the batting won't catch as you quilt.

5. Stitch the tote front and back together, with right sides facing, along the sides and the bottom edges to make the outer bag. Leave the top edge unstitched. Clip the corners of the seam allowance of the outer bag close to but not through the stitching. Leave it inside out.

6. To pleat the bag bottom, flatten the bag so that one side seam is aligned with the bottom seam of the bag (figure 11–13a). Stitch across the resulting triangular point 1″ from the tip of the point (11–13b). Repeat with the other point. Turn the outer bag right-side out. It will look like 11–13c. Set it aside.

7. For the bag lining, place the two remaining 14½ × 16½″ pieces of floral print fabric together, right sides facing. Stitch along the sides and across the bottom, leaving a 6″ opening at the bottom edges for turning (figure 11–14). Leave the top edge unstitched

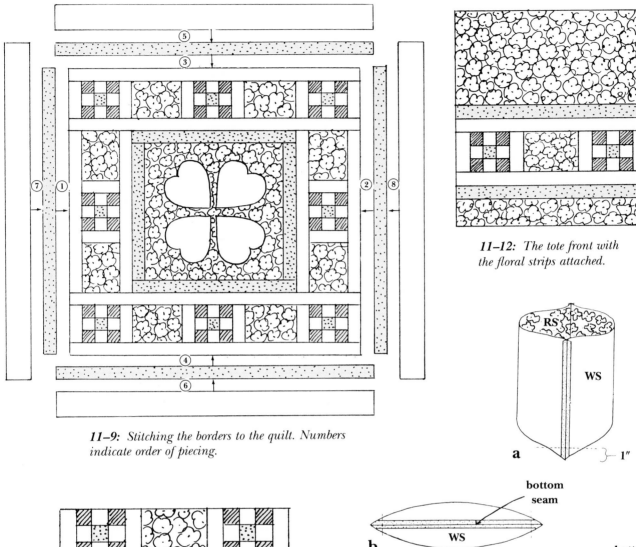

11–9: Stitching the borders to the quilt. Numbers indicate order of piecing.

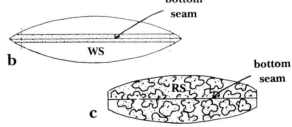

11–12: The tote front with the floral strips attached.

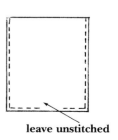

11–13: Pleating the tote bag. **a:** Stitch across the point 1″ from the tip. **b:** Bottom view of the bag, wrong side out, showing placement of stitching. **c:** Bottom view, right side out. The lining is pleated the same way.

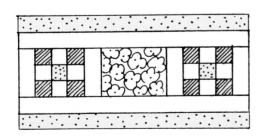

11–10: A pieced row for the tote front.

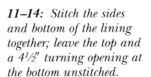

11–11: A pieced row with tan and pink strips added, used in the tote front.

11–14: Stitch the sides and bottom of the lining together; leave the top and a 4½″ turning opening at the bottom unstitched.

leave unstitched

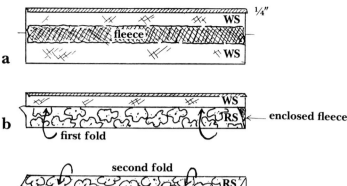

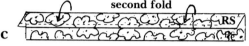

11–15: Making handles. **a:** *Fold under ¼″ of fabric to the wrong side as a hem.* **b:** *Fold up the unfolded side over the fleece.* **c:** *Fold down the hemmed edge and stitch through all layers (dashed line).*

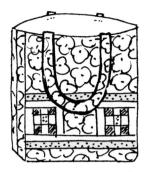

11–16: Baste the handles to the right side of the outer bag, 3½″ in from the side seams, with raw edges aligned.

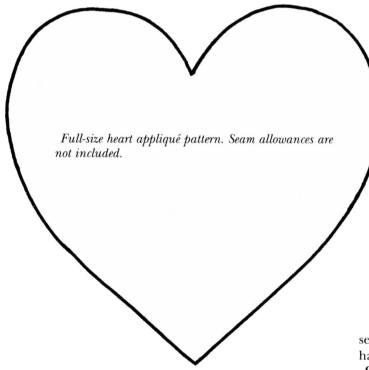

Full-size heart appliqué pattern. Seam allowances are not included.

11–17: Place the outer bag inside the inner bag, with right sides together.

also. Pleat the bottom of the lining as you did the outer bag.

8. To make the handles, center one of the 1 × 18″ strips of fleece on the wrong side of a 3½ × 18½″ floral print strip and baste the fleece in place. Press a ¼″ hem on one long edge of the floral print fabric (figure 11–15a). Then fold up the other long edge of the floral strip to cover the fleece strip (11–15b). Fold the side with the hem over the fleece strip, completely enclosing it. Stitch along the center of the strip to secure the layers (figure 11–15c). This completes one handle. Make the second handle the same way.

9. Baste the handles to the outer tote bag 3½″ in from the side seams (figure 11–16). The raw edges of the bag top and the handles should be aligned. Place the outer bag inside the lining bag with right sides facing (figure 11–17), align the seams, and baste and stitch the bags together along the top edge. Turn the tote bag right-side out through the opening in the bottom of the lining. Hand stitch the turning opening closed.

10. Stitch around the top edge of the tote bag, ¼″ down from the edge. Stitch again ¼″ down from the first line of stitching. This will keep the bag layers from shifting during use.

Yummy Treats Placemat Set

Do your kids eat like animals? Serve up their meals on dogbone placemats and perhaps it will be just the reminder they need to behave like little ladies and gentlemen—but, then again, maybe not! After all, kids will be kids! Choose bright colors for the fabrics, and hand-stitch the ''YUMMY'' in black pearl cotton using a simple running stitch. Finished size of each placemat: 19 × 14″.

Materials for Two Placemats

- ¾ yard black-and-white checked fabric (includes enough for backings)
- ¼ yard solid green fabric
- ½ yard solid off-white fabric
- ¼ yard red print fabric
- 4 yards of red piping
- Two 20 × 15″ pieces of low-loft quilt batting or fleece
- Thread to match fabrics
- Black pearl cotton or 6-strand floss for embroidery

Directions

Construction is done with right sides of fabric facing and seam allowances of ¼″, which are included in the given measurements.

1. Cut all pieces as listed in the cutting guides.

2. Look at the construction diagram (figure 12–1). We need some two-triangle squares, which we will make by a speed method. Take a 5 × 7″ piece of off-white fabric and green fabric. Draw six 1⅞″ squares on the wrong side of the off-white piece and pin the fabric together with the green piece, right sides facing. Draw diagonal lines through the squares. Stitch ¼″ from each side of the diagonal lines as shown in figure 12–2a. Cut apart the squares along the marked lines through both layers of fabric, and cut each square along the diagonal line also (figure 12–2b). Press open each of the triangles to form a 2-triangle square, as shown in figure 12–2c. You will have twelve 2-triangle squares.

3. Stitch a two-triangle square on each of two

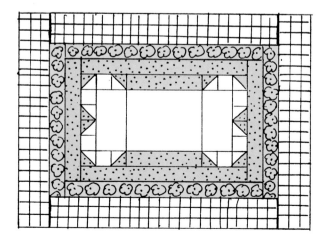

12–1: Construction diagram for the YUMMY placemat.

Black-and-white checked fabric cutting guide

Four	2½ × 15½″ (border)
Four	2½ × 14½″ (border)
Two	14½ × 19½″ (backing)

Green fabric cutting guide

One	5 × 7″
Four	1½ × 5½″
Four	1½ × 11½″
Four	1½ × 8½″

Off-white fabric cutting guide

One	5 × 7″
Sixteen	1½ × 1½″
Four	4½ × 2½″
Two	4½ × 5½″

Red print fabric cutting guide

Four	1½ × 13½″
Four	1½ × 10½″

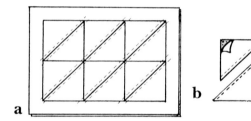

12–2. **a:** *Marking and stitching for two-triangle squares.* **b:** *Cutting the pieces apart on the diagonals.* **c:** *The finished two-triangle square.*

opposite sides of a 1½″ off-white square, as shown in figure 12–3, to make a 3-square unit. Make 8 of these 3-square units (4 per placemat). Press. Set them aside.

4. Take two 2-triangle squares and two 1½″ off-white squares and stitch them together as shown in figure 12–4 to make a 4-square unit. Make a total of four of the 4-square units (2 per placemat). Press.

5. Take a 4½ × 2½″ off-white rectangle. Stitch the 4-square unit to it on its long side. Then stitch a 3-square unit to each short side (figure 12–5) to make a "bone end." Make 3 more of these bone ends (2 per placemat).

6. Take a 4½ × 5½″ off-white rectangle and two green 1½ × 5½″ strips. Stitch one green strip to each long side of the off-white rectangle as shown in figure 12–6. Press. This makes a bone center. Make one more bone center the same way.

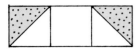

12–3: A 3-square unit.

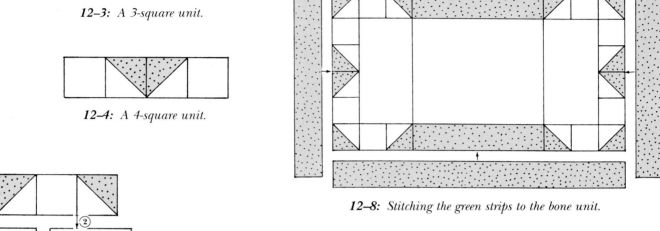

12–8: Stitching the green strips to the bone unit.

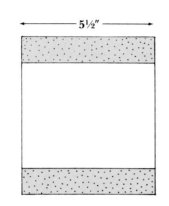

12–4: A 4-square unit.

12–5: Making a bone end. Numbers indicate order of piecing.

12–6: Stitch the green strips to the off-white rectangle for the bone center.

5½″

them to the short ends of the bone unit to complete the placemat center (figure 12–8). Repeat for the second placemat.

9. Refer to figure 12–9 for steps 9 and 10. Stitch a red 1½ × 13½″ strip to each of the long sides of a placemat center. Stitch a 1½ × 10½″ red strip to each of the short ends. Repeat for the second placemat. Press.

10. Stitch a 2½ × 15½″ black-and-white checked strip to each long side of the placemat. Stitch a 2½ × 14½″ black-and-white checked strip to each short side. Stitch the four border strips to the second placemat the same way. Press. This completes the placemat tops.

11. Transfer the YUMMY letters to the center of each placemat.

12. Baste the batting to the wrong side of each placemat. Trim away the excess batting. Baste the piping to the front of each placemat, with its raw edge aligned with the placemat's raw edges (see general directions on piping, if necessary).

13. Stitch a checked 14½ × 19½″ backing piece to the placemat front, with right sides facing, along all 4 sides, leaving a 5″ opening along one long edge for turning. Clip the corners of the seam allowances and turn the placemat right-side out. Repeat for the second placemat.

14. Hand-stitch the turning openings closed. Pin-baste the layers of each placemat in a few places (or hand-baste if you prefer) and machine-quilt the placemats as desired.

15. Hand embroider the YUMMY in the pearl cotton, using one strand and a running stitch. (If you have 6-strand embroidery floss, use three strands of the 6-strand floss in your needle instead of the pearl cotton.)

7. Stitch two bone ends to each bone center, as shown in figure 12–7, to make a bone unit. Make another the same way. Press.

8. Take two green 1½ × 11½″ strips and stitch one to each long side of the finished bone unit (figure 12–8). Take two green 1½ × 8½″ strips and stitch

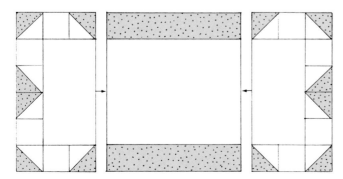

12–7: Stitch two bone ends to a bone center.

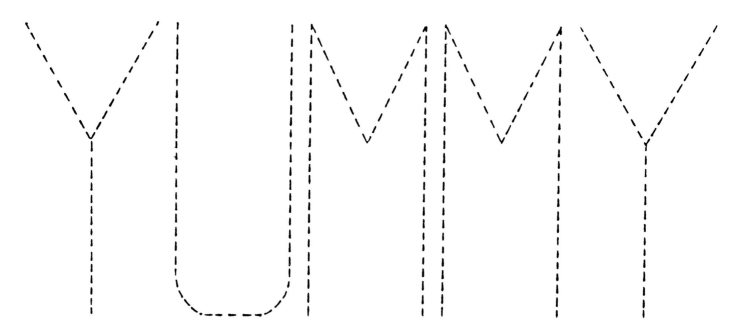

Full-sized YUMMY embroidery pattern.

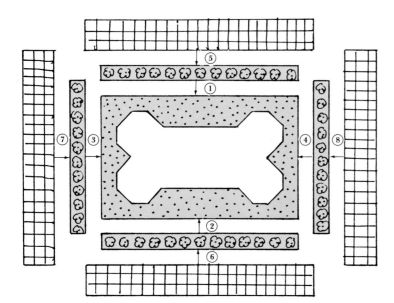

12–9: Stitching the borders to the center. Numbers
indicate the order of piecing.

The Buzz of the Bees Wall Hanging

Bees buzzing and flying in a graceful pattern, searching for the next flower to visit: What a fun theme for a wall hanging! Machine straight-stitch helps define the wings, while satin stitch embroidery forms the antennas and the stingers. Finished size of the wall hanging: 26 × 26″. Finished bee block size: 10 × 10″.

Materials

- ¾ yard white fabric with green print (referred to as "green" or G in the directions); a vine pattern was used in the model
- ⅓ yard solid white fabric (W)
- ⅓ yard black fabric (B)
- ⅓ yard yellow fabric (Y)
- 28 × 28″ piece of quilt batting
- 28 × 28″ piece of fabric for the quilt backing
- All-purpose threads to match the fabrics
- 4 yards of double-fold white quilt binding (½″ folded, 2″ unfolded)
- If you will do hand embroidery, 1 skein of black 6-strand embroidery floss

Directions

Construction is done with right sides of fabric facing and seam allowances of ¼″, which are included in all of the given measurements. The bee blocks are constructed in nine rows (see block diagram, figure 13–1). You will need 4 of each row for the quilt center.

1. Cut out all the pieces of fabric listed in the cutting guides.

2. For row 2: Stitch an 8 × 5″ green (G) rectangle on its long side to each long side of a 1½ × 8″ black (B) strip and press. You now have a GBG rectangle. Cut across the GBG rectangle to make four 1½″-wide GBG strips, one for row 2 of each block (figure 13–2). Set them aside.

3. For row 3: Stitch one 8 × 4½″ green piece on its long side to each long side of an 8 × 2½″ yellow strip. You now have a GYG rectangle, as shown in figure 13–3. Cut across the GYG rectangle to make four 1½″-wide GYG strips. Each will become row 3 of the bee block. Set them aside.

4. For row 4: Stitch one 8 × 3½″ green piece on its long side to each of the long sides of an 8 × 4½″ black piece, to make a GBG rectangle. Cut across the GBG rectangle to make four 1½″-wide GBG strips, as shown in Figure 13–4. Set them aside.

5. For row 5: Take one 8 × 3½″ yellow piece and two 8 × 4″ green pieces. Stitch an 8 × 4″ green piece

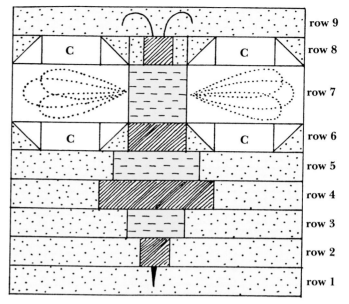

13–1: Block assembly diagram for a bee block.

Closeup of block.

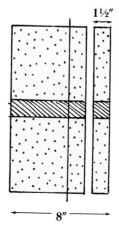

13–2: Making row 2. Cut 1½″ wide strips across the assembled pieces as shown.

Green-printed white fabric cutting guide

Quantity and Size		Use
Eight	1½ × 10½″	row 1 and row 9
Two	8 × 5″	row 2
Two	8 × 4½″	row 3
Two	8 × 3½″	row 4
Two	8 × 4″	row 5
One	9 × 5″	A squares
Two	8 × 1″	row 8
Two	1½ × 22″*	inner border
Two	1½ × 24″*	inner border
Four	1½ × 1½″	outer border corner
Four	1½ × 2½″	border corner

*Borders will be trimmed shorter later.

Solid white fabric cutting guide

Quantity and Size		Use
One	9 × 5″	A squares
Sixteen	1½ × 2½″	C strip (rows 6 and 8)
Two	16 × 4½″	row 7

Black fabric cutting guide

Quantity and Size		Use
Two	1½ × 8″	row 2 and 8
One	8 × 4½″	row 4
Four	1½ × 2½″	row 6
Four	1½ × 22½″	border

Yellow fabric cutting guide

Quantity and Size		Use
One	2½″ × 8″	row 3
One	3½″ × 8″	row 5
One	2½″ × 16″	row 7
Four	1½ × 22½″	border
Four	1½ × 1½″	border corner

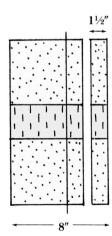

13–3: Making row 3. Cut across the assembled pieces as shown.

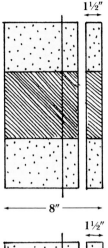

13–4: Making row 4. Cut across the assembled pieces as shown.

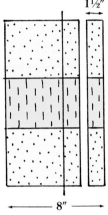

13–5: Making row 5. Cut across the assembled pieces as shown.

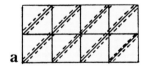

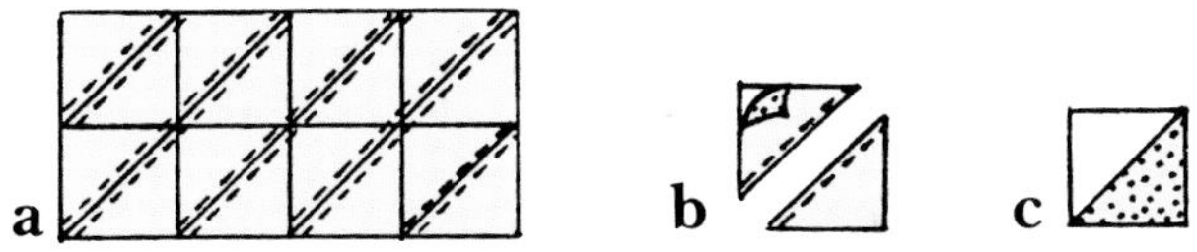

13–6: Speed piecing and cutting 2-triangle A squares.
a: *Marking and stitching.* **b:** *Cutting the two-triangle squares.* **c:** *Two-triangle square pressed open.*

on its long side to each long side of an 8 × 3½″ yellow piece, to make a GYG rectangle. Cut across the GYG rectangle to make four 1½″-wide GYG strips, as shown in Figure 13–5. Each will become row 5 of a bee block. Set them aside.

6. For row 6: We will make some two-triangle squares using speed methods, from solid white and green-printed fabric. Take a piece of solid white fabric 9 × 5″ and a piece of green fabric the same size. Draw eight 1⅞″ squares on the wrong side of the green fabric. Draw a diagonal line through each square, as shown in figure 13–6a. Pin the green rectangle and the solid white (W) rectangle together, right sides facing. On both sides of the ruled diagonal lines, stitch ¼″ away as shown in figure 13–6a. Cut through both layers of fabric along the ruled square lines and along the diagonal lines as shown in figure 13–6b. Each two-fabric unit, when pressed open, is a

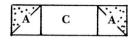

13–7: An ACA unit for row 6 or 8.

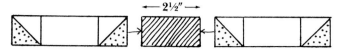

13–8: *Assembly of row 6, with ACA units on the outside.*

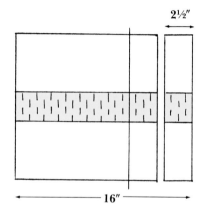

13–9: Assembly and cutting of row 7.

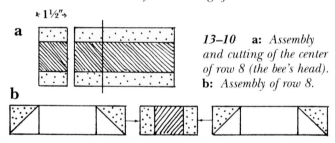

13–10   a: *Assembly and cutting of the center of row 8 (the bee's head).* **b:** *Assembly of row 8.*

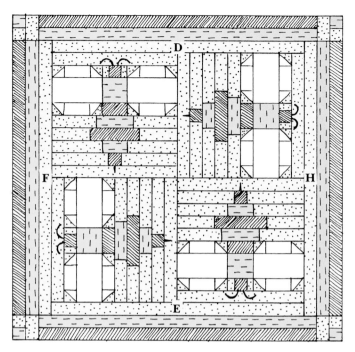

13–11: *Diagram showing the completed quilt top.*

two-triangle A square. You should have 16 A squares. Take a white 1½ × 2½" (C) strip. Stitch one A square to each short side of the C strip, as shown in figure 13–7. Make 16 of these ACA units. Set them aside. From the black fabric, take a 1½ × 2½" strip and stitch it between two of the ACA units to make row 6 (figure 13–8). Repeat to make a total of four of row 6. You will have eight ACA units left over for use in row 8. Set them all aside.

7. To make row 7: Stitch one solid white (W) 16 × 4½" piece on its long side to each long side of a yellow 2½ × 16" strip, as shown in figure 13–9, to make a WYW rectangle. Cut across the WYW rectangle to make four 2½"-wide strips. Each will become row 7 of the bee block. Set them aside.

8. For row 8: Take one black 1½ × 8" strip and two 8 × 1" green strips. Stitch each green strip on a long side to each long side of the black strip to make a GBG strip (figure 13–10a). Cut across the GBG strip

to make four 1½" wide GBG pieces. Stitch one of these GBG units between two ACA units left over from step 6, as shown in figure 13–10b to make row 8 of the bee block. Make 4 of row 8.

9. Row 1 and row 9 are each 1½" × 10½" G strips. You need 4 of each row.

10. To assemble the block, stitch row 1 to row 2 on a long side, with right sides of fabric facing; stitch row 3 to row 2, and continue on adding row by row to make a bee block. Check the construction diagram (Figure 13–1) for reference. Make a total of 4 bee blocks.

11. Referring to the completed quilt diagram (figure 13–11), stitch the 4 blocks together to form the quilt center, rotating the blocks as shown to make the design. Press.

Borders

12. Take two green strips 1½" wide and 22" long and trim them to the same length as your quilt center, measuring down the center of the quilt (about 20½"). Stitch these strips to two opposite sides of the quilt center (see figure 13–11; these are borders D and E). Then measure the width of your quilt center, including the width of the D and E borders you just attached. Trim the two 1½" × 24" green border strips to the size you just measured (about 22½") for border strips F and H, and stitch one border strip to each of the two remaining sides of the quilt center (see figure 13–11). Press.

13. Border 2: Take the four yellow 1½" × 24" border

strips and the four black 1½″ × 24″ strips. Stitch one black strip to one yellow strip on its long side. These are the BY border units; make 4 of them. Press. Measure the length of your quilt center from the top to the bottom, measuring down the center of the quilt. Trim all four of the BY border units to that length (about 22½″). Stitch one BY border unit to each of two opposite sides of the quilt center as shown in figure 13–12 (left and right sides), reserving the remaining two BY strips. Set the quilt center aside.

14. To make a corner unit of the outer border, take a 1½″ square of yellow fabric and one the same size of green fabric. Also take a 1½ × 2½″ green rectangle. Stitch a yellow square to a green square, and then add a green rectangle on the long side, to form a corner unit, as shown in figure 13–13. Make a total of 4 corner units the same way.

15. Stitch one corner unit to each short end of the two BY border strips you reserved earlier. See figure 13–14 for positioning of corners. Next, stitch a border with corners to each of the two remaining sides of the quilt center and press (figure 13–12).

16. Transfer the wing markings and the antenna markings to the bee blocks. Machine satin stitch along the antennas and satin stitch a stinger on the back end of the bee, using a stabilizer such as a piece of tracing paper pinned to the wrong side of the fabric for ease of stitching or tear-away stabilizer. Or, if you prefer, use 3 strands of black embroidery thread and hand embroider the wings and antennas.

Stem stitch for antennas.

17. To assemble the quilt, tape the backing fabric wrong-side up to your work surface, center the batting over the backing fabric, and center the quilt top face up over the batting. Hand-baste or pin-baste the layers together to prepare it for machine quilting. Machine quilt or hand quilt as desired. Straight-stitch along the markings on the wings in black thread by machine or by hand.

18. After quilting, baste about ½″ in from the raw edges of the quilt top all around and trim away the excess batting and backing that extends beyond the quilt top. Bind the quilt to complete it (see general instructions for binding details).

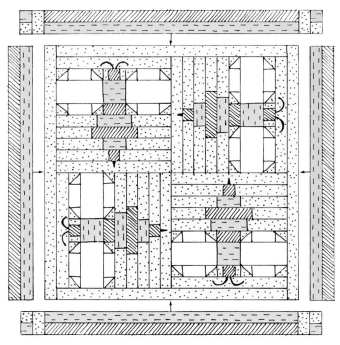

13–12: Attaching the black-yellow outer borders.

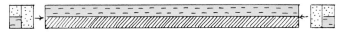

13–13: A corner unit for the outer border.

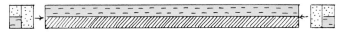

13–14: Attaching corner units to a BY border strip.

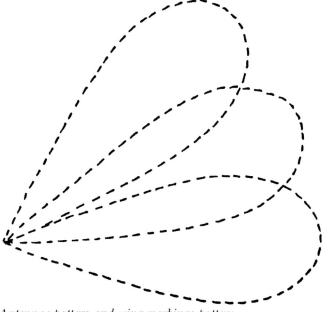

Antennae pattern and wing markings pattern.

Spring-on-the-Square Quilt and Pillows

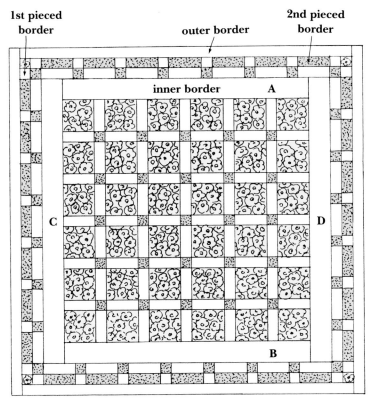

1st pieced border

outer border

2nd pieced border

inner border

A

C

D

B

14–1: Construction diagram for quilt.

A large-scale floral pattern adds lively interest to the large squares in these projects, while the teal border is reminiscent of a cross-stitched design. Two colorful pillows carry out the motif. You can make the quilt in just a few hours, because it is so simple. Finished quilt: 33 × 33″. Finished size of the pillows: each is 14 × 14″.

Materials for All Projects

- ¾ yard large-scale floral print fabric
- 1¼ yard off-white fabric
- ¾ yard teal blue print fabric
- 35 × 35″ piece of low-loft batting for the quilt
- Two 15 × 15″ pieces of quilt batting (one for each pillow)
- 35 × 35″ piece of fabric for the quilt backing
- Two 15 × 15″ pieces of muslin (one for each pillow)
- Two 15 × 15″ pieces of backing fabric (one for each pillow)
- 4 yards of piping (2 yards of piping for each pillow)
- 4 yards of double-fold quilt binding (folded width ½″; unfolded width, 2″)
- All-purpose threads to match the fabrics

Large floral print fabric cutting guide

Quantity and Size		Use
Three	3½ × 44″	floral block rows
Ten	3½ × 3½″	quilt row ends; 4-block pillow
Four	1½ × 1½″	quilt corner
One	6½ × 6½″	1-block pillow
Two	2½ × 10½″	1-block pillow
Three	2½ × 14½	1-block pillow

Off-white fabric cutting guide

Quantity and Size		Use
Five	1½ × 44″	quilt
Three	3½ × 44″	quilt
Twelve	1½ × 3½″	quilt; 4-block pillow
Two	2½ × 23½″	quilt inner border
Two	2½ × 27½″	quilt inner border
Four	1½ × 1½″	quilt corners
Two	1½ × 31½″	quilt outer border
Two	1½ × 33½″	quilt outer border
Two	1½ × 7½″	4-block pillow
Two	1½ × 9½″	4-block pillow
Four	1½ × 6½″	1-block pillow
Two	1½ × 8½″	1-block pillow
Two	1½ × 10½″	1-block pillow

Teal print fabric cutting guide

Quantity and Size		Use
Three	1½ × 44″	quilt
Seven	1½ × 1½″	quilt and pillows
Two	3½ × 44″	quilt border
Two	3 × 9½″	4-block pillow
Two	3 × 14½″	4-block pillow

Directions

Construction is done with right sides of fabric facing and seam allowances of ¼″, which are included in all of the given measurements. The quilt center is made of 6 block rows and 5 sashing rows (see figure 14–1).

The Quilt

Making the Block Rows

1. Cut out all the pieces needed for your project (either just the quilt pieces or the quilt and pillows

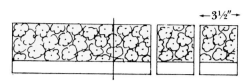

14–2: Cutting A units.

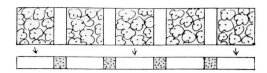

14–6: Stitching a horizontal sashing strip to a floral block row.

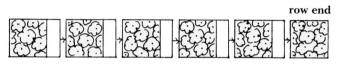

14–3: Making a floral block row: 5 A units plus a row end.

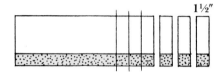

14–4: Cutting B units.

14–5: A horizontal sashing strip, made from 5 B units plus an off-white end unit.

pieces, if you prefer to cut them all at once).

2. Stitch a floral print 3½ × 44″ strip on its long side to an off-white fabric 1½ × 44″ strip. Press. Make two more two-strip units the same way. Take each two-strip unit and cut across it to make 3½″-wide A units (figure 14–2). You will need 30 A units for the quilt. Set them aside.

3. Referring to figure 14–3, stitch together 5 A units, adding a 3½″ floral square at the right of the last A unit, to make a floral row. Make a total of six of these rows. Set them aside.

Making the Horizontal Sashing Rows

4. Stitch one off-white 3½ × 44″ strip to a teal 1½ × 44″ strip on a long side. Make two more 2-strip units the same way. Press. Take a two-strip unit and cut across both strips to make nineteen 1½″-wide B units (see figure 14–4). Cut another nineteen 1½″-wide B units from the second two-strip unit. Cut eighteen B units from the third two-strip unit. You will have a total of 56 B units.

5. Stitch together 5 B units on their short sides, as shown in figure 14–5; at the end of this add a 1½ × 3½″ off-white strip. This completes one horizontal sashing row. Make a total of 5 horizontal sashing rows in the same way.

6. To assemble the quilt center, attach a floral row to a horizontal sashing row as shown in figure 14–6. Continue adding floral block strips, alternating with sashing strips, to complete the quilt center (a total of six floral block strips and five horizontal sashing strips; see figure 14–1, the construction diagram, for reference). Press.

Borders, Quilting, and Binding

Refer to figure 14–7 for attachment of all borders (steps 7 through 13).

7. Stitch one off-white border strip (2½ × 23½″) to the top of the quilt center and the second to the bottom of the quilt center (A and B in figure 14–7). Stitch your 2½ × 27″ off-white border strips to the sides of your quilt center for the side inner border strips, C and D in figure 14–7. Press.

8. To make the first pieced border strip, make a row by stitching together 6 B units as shown in figure 14–8, along with one off-white 1½ × 3½″ strip. Press. Make another first pieced border strip the same way. Stitch these strips to the top and bottom of the quilt center and press (see figure 14–1 for reference). Set the unit aside.

9. Stitch together 7 B units, adding a 1½″ teal end square at the end, as shown in figure 14–9, to make the top first pieced border (G in figure 14–7). Stitch another 7 B units and teal square together to make the bottom first pieced border (H in 14–7). Stitch them to the top and bottom of the quilt center. Press. Set the unit aside.

Making the Second Pieced Border

10. Stitch an off-white 1½ × 44″ strip on its long side to the long side of a teal 3½ × 44″ strip. Make another 2-strip unit the same way. Press. Cut across the two-strip units to make twenty-eight 1½″-wide C units (see figure 14–10).

11. Stitch together 7 C units along with one off-white 1½″ square, as shown in figure 14–11. Press. Make another strip the same way. These will become second pieced border strips (I and J in figure 14–7). Stitch them to the right and left sides of the quilt center unit made in step 9. Press. Set it aside.

12. Stitch 7 C units together, adding a 1½″ off-white

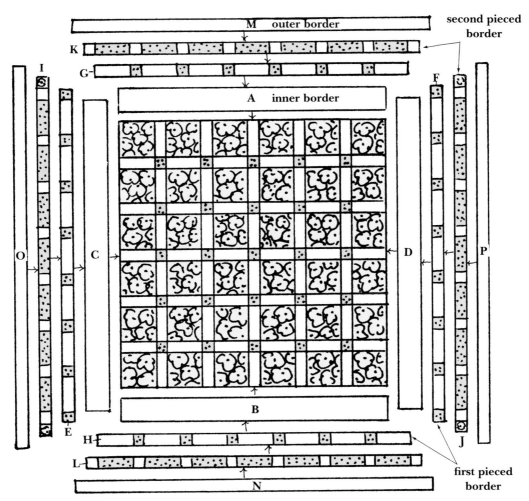

14–7: Diagram showing attachment of the borders, from A to M.

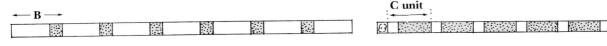

14–8: An E or F first pieced border strip, made of 6 B units plus an end unit.

14–9: G or H first pieced border strips: 7 B units plus a teal square end unit.

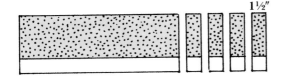

14–10: Cutting the C units.

14–11: An I or J second pieced border strip: 7 C units plus a white square end unit.

14–12: K or L second pieced border strip: 7 C units, a floral square on the left, and white and floral squares on the right.

square to the teal end. Press. Stitch one of the floral 1½″ squares to each end of the strip you just made (see figure 14–12). Make another strip the same way and press both. These will be the K and L border strips (see figure 14–7). Stitch them to the top and bottom of the quilt center unit made in step 11. Press.

Outer border

13. Take two 1½ × 31½″ off-white strips for the outer border. They are border strips M and N in figure 14–7. Stitch them to the top and bottom of the quilt center unit you made in step 12. Take two off-white 1½ × 33½″ strips and stitch them to the remaining two sides of the quilt center unit (border strips O and

P in figure 14–7). Press. The finished quilt top will look like figure 14–1.

Basting, Quilting, and Binding

14. Tape the 35 × 35″ backing fabric, right side down, to your work surface. Center the batting over the backing fabric, and center the quilt top, right-side up, over the batting. Hand-baste or pin-baste the layers together. Machine quilt or hand quilt the project, as you desire (see general instructions for basting and quilting information).

15. After quilting, baste around the raw edges of the quilt top, about ½″ in from the raw edge. Trim away any excess batting and backing fabric that extend beyond the edge of the quilt top. Bind the quilt to complete it (see general instructions for binding information).

The 4-Block Pillow (figure 14–13)

1. Cut four 3½″ squares of floral fabric, one 1½″ square of teal fabric, and four 1½ × 3½″ strips of off-white fabric, if you have not already done so. Stitch a floral square to either side of a strip of off-white fabric on its 3½″ sides (figure 14–14a) to make a block row. Make another block row the same way. Set them aside.

2. Make a central sashing strip by sewing two off-white strips (1½ × 3½″) to either side of a teal square (figure 14–14b). Press.

3. Stitch a block row to the top of the sashing strip and one to the bottom of the sashing strip to make the pillow center, as shown in figure 14–14c.

4. From the off-white fabric, cut two 1½ × 7½″ strips if you haven't already done so, and stitch them to two opposite sides of the pillow center (A and B in figure 14–15). Cut two strips 1½ × 9½″ from the off-white fabric, if you haven't already done so, and stitch them to the remaining two sides of the pillow center (they are C and D in 14–15) to complete the inner border.

5. From the teal fabric, cut two 3″ × 9½″ strips, if you have not already done so, and stitch them to the top and bottom of the quilt center (E and F in figure 14–15). Cut two 3″ × 14½″ teal strips and stitch them to the remaining sides (G and H in figure 14–15). Press. The finished pillow top looks like 14–13.

6. Tape a 15 × 15″ muslin square to your work surface and center the batting over it. Center the pillow top over the batting square, right side up, and baste the three layers together. Quilt the pillow top as desired. Then baste about ¼″ in from the raw edges of the pillow top all around and trim away any excess batting and muslin that extend beyond the pillow top. Baste the piping around the edges of the pillow top,

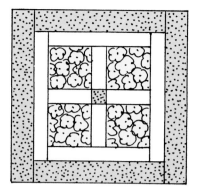

14–13: Construction diagram of the 4-block pillow.

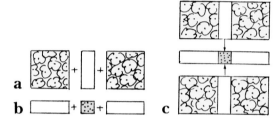

14–14: 4-block pillow construction. **a:** *joining two blocks to an off-white strip to make a row.* **b:** *Joining two off-white strips to a teal square to make a sashing strip.* **c:** *The two block rows stitched to the sashing strip.*

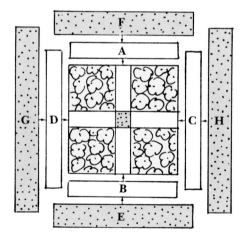

14–15: Adding the inner and outer borders, 4-block pillow.

with the raw edges facing out (see general directions for piping instructions).

7. Take the backing fabric and stitch the backing fabric to the pillow top, right sides facing, along all sides, leaving a 10″ opening along one edge for turning. Clip the corners of the seam allowances for ease of turning and turn the pillow covering right-side out. Insert the pillow form and hand-stitch the turning opening closed to finish the first pillow.

14–16: Construction diagram of the one-block pillow.

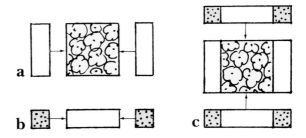

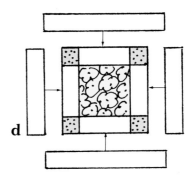

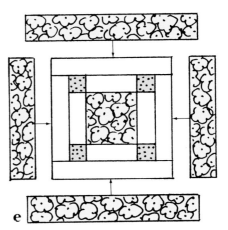

One-Block Pillow (figure 14–16)

1. If you haven't already cut these when you cut your quilt pieces, cut the following: Floral fabric: one 6½″ square, two 2½ × 10½″ strips, and two 2½ × 14½″ strips. Off-white fabric: four 1½ × 6½″ strips, two 1½ × 8½″ strips, and two 1½ × 10½″ strips. Teal: four 1½″ squares.

2. Stitch a 1½ × 6½″ off-white strip to the left side of the floral square and one to the right side (figure 14–17a). Set it aside.

3. Stitch a 1½ × 6½″ off-white strip between two teal squares to make a top inner border for the center square (figure 14–17b). Repeat for the bottom border, and stitch the borders in place on the unit made in step 2 (figure 14–17c). Press.

4. For the middle border, take the two off-white 1½ × 8½″ strips and stitch them to opposite sides of the pillow center unit made in step 3. Take the two 1½ × 10½″ off-white strips and stitch them to the remaining two sides to complete the inner border (figure 14–17d). Press.

5. For the outer border, take the two 2½ × 10½″ floral strips and stitch them to opposite sides of the pillow center (see figure 14–17e). Press. Take the two 2½ × 14½″ floral strips and stitch them to the remaining 2 sides of the pillow center. Press. This completes the pillow top.

6. Quilt and finish the pillow by the same procedure you used for the 4-block pillow (see steps 6 and 7 of the 4-block pillow instructions).

14–17: One-block pillow construction. **a:** Joining two off-white inner border strips to a floral block.
b: Joining two teal squares to an off-white strip.
c: Attaching the top and bottom inner borders.
d: Attaching the second border strips. **e:** Attaching the third (floral) border strips.

Trailing Ivy Placemat and Napkin Set

A set of these mats and napkins would make a lovely wedding shower gift. Although the model is off-white and green, you can choose any color combination that pleases you for the fabrics and thread. Finished sizes: placemat, 11 × 17″; napkin, 18 × 18″.

I used a store-bought placemat, napkin, and apron to create this set, which makes it a very fast project to complete. I've given instructions for making the placemat and napkin from scratch if you prefer to make them yourself, however. An undecorated apron can be made from a commercial apron pattern, if you prefer not to buy a finished apron. Remember to prewash and dry any mats, napkins, or aprons you buy, as well as the fabrics, and be sure they all are colorfast before you start appliquéing.

Materials for One Placemat, One Napkin, and an Apron*

- Scraps of three or four different green fabrics, totaling about ¼ yard
- 12 × 12″ piece of fusible transfer webbing (enough for a napkin and placemat)**
- 14 × 14″ piece of fusible transfer webbing for apron**
- All-purpose threads to match the green fabrics**
- Green hand-sewing thread if you will do hand appliqué
- Green 6-strand embroidery floss for vines if you will do hand embroidery
- 18 × 18″ finished cloth table napkin *or* one 19 × 19″ piece of fabric to make your own napkin
- Store-bought placemat, 11 × 17″, *or* 2 pieces of off-white fabric, 11½ × 17½″ each
- 11½ × 17½″ piece of fleece or low-loft batting for the placemat
- Off-white sewing thread
- 1 apron (purchased or made by you from any commercial pattern—follow yardage on pattern for fabric)*
- 6 × 6″ piece of tear-away stabilizer or sheet of tracing paper

*If you are making the apron yourself, add the apron yardage given on your commercial pattern to the amount of fabric you need to buy.
**Needed if you will do machine appliqué.

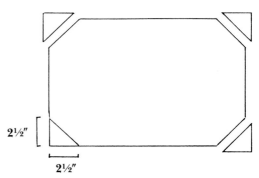

15–1: *For the placemat, mark the corner triangles and trim them off.*

Directions

Construction is done with right sides of fabric facing, unless otherwise noted, and seam allowances of ¼″. Appliqué patterns are drawn without seam allowances in the book; seam allowances are not needed for machine appliqué. If you've never worked with fusible transfer webbing before, you might want to read about it in the general directions section of the book. For hand appliqué, add ³⁄₁₆″ seam allowances around all appliqué patterns as you cut them out, and follow the steps labeled "H" below instead of "M" below. See the hand appliqué instructions in the general directions section of the book also.

Placemat

1. If you are making your own placemat, mark a triangle with 2½″ sides at each corner of one of the off-white 11½ × 17½″ pieces of fabric and trim off the triangles (see figure 15–1).
2. Baste the batting or fleece to the wrong side of the piece made in step 1. Trim the excess batting from the corners. Place this fleeced section against the remaining 11½ × 17½″ piece of fabric, with right sides of the two fabric pieces facing, and secure them together with pins. Trim away the remaining corner areas from the unfleeced piece of fabric.
3. Referring to figure 15–2, stitch around all sides of the placemat, ¼″ in from the raw edges, but leave a 6″ opening along one of the long edges for turning. Trim the excess seam allowance away at the corners of the placemat, so the mat will lie flat, and turn it right-side out.
4. Hand-stitch the turning opening closed. Press the placemat, and then pin-baste or hand-baste through all three layers. Machine quilt the placemat ⅛″ in from the edges, and again ¼″ in from the first line of stitching.

5M. *For machine appliqué,* trace a total of 6 to 8 reversed leaves of various sizes of leaves onto the paper side of fusible transfer webbing. Roughly cut out the leaves from the webbing. Fuse the webbing leaves to the wrong sides of assorted scraps of the green fabrics with a warm iron, and carefully cut the leaves out of the fabrics. Peel off the paper from the webbing side of the leaves. Arrange the leaves in a pleasing manner on the placemat front (see figure 15–3 for guidance, if necessary). Fuse the leaves in place.

5H. *For hand appliqué,* trace 6 or 8 leaves to the right side of assorted scraps of green fabric and cut them out, adding ³⁄₁₆″ seam allowance around all leaves as you cut. See the general directions section of the book for more information about preparing hand appliqués. Pin or baste the leaves to the placemat top in a pleasing design (see figure 15–2 for guidance, if necessary). Stitch the leaves to the placemat with green hand sewing thread and tiny tacking stitches or, if you prefer, choose a decorative stitch like the button hole stitch.

6. Draw the vines and tendrils freehand on the placemat using a water-soluble marking pencil. Be creative and don't worry about perfection, as these vines are supposed to look as though they are meandering along!

7. Machine appliqué the leaves in place through all three layers of the placemat, using matching colors of thread and a medium-width machine satin stitch. Narrow the width of the satin stitch slightly to satin stitch along the vine and tendril markings. If you prefer hand embroidery, embroider the vines using the stem stitch and 3 strands of embroidery floss.

Napkin

1. If you are making your own napkin, turn under ¼″ TWICE around all 4 sides of the 19 × 19″ square of fabric to make a double hem, and secure the hem in place with matching thread and a hemstitch or machine blindstitch. Press. You now have an 18 × 18″ napkin.

2M. If you are going to do *machine appliqué,* trace the leaf for the napkin (see the appliqué pattern) onto the paper side of the fusible webbing, cut the leaf roughly out of the webbing, and fuse the webbing leaf to the wrong side of one of the green scraps of fabric. Carefully cut the leaf out of the fabric, peel off the paper, and fuse the leaf to one corner of the napkin on the right side of the fabric. Draw the vine lines freehand on the napkin. Satin-stitch the leaf and the vines as you did for the placemat, adding stabilizer underneath for ease of stitching. You now have a

15–2: Stitch around the sides of the placemat, ¼″ in from the edges, leaving a turning opening.

15–3: Placement diagram for the appliqués on the placemat.

complete napkin. Now, wasn't that just too easy?

2H. *For hand appliqué,* trace the leaf for the napkin onto the front of a scrap of green fabric, and cut out the leaf, adding ³⁄₁₆″ seam allowances as you cut. Refer to the hand appliqué instructions in the general directions section of the book if necessary to prepare the appliqué. Baste the leaf in place on the napkin front. Appliqué the leaf in place, using hand sewing thread if possible, and tiny tacking stitches. Draw the vines freehand and embroider them using 3 strands of green embroidery thread and the stem stitch.

Apron

1M. If you want to do *machine appliqué,* trace 6 leaves of varying sizes onto the paper side of fusible transfer webbing and cut them out roughly from the webbing. Fuse the webbing leaves to the wrong sides of scraps of several shades of green fabric with a warm iron. Carefully cut out the leaves from the fabric, remove the paper from the webbing, and arrange them at the top of the apron; see figure 15–4 for placement suggestions. Fuse the leaves in place.

1H. If you prefer to do *hand appliqué*, trace 6 leaves of varying sizes onto the right sides of scraps of several shades of green fabric, and cut them out, adding seam allowances of ³⁄₁₆″ as you cut around each pattern. See the general directions section of the book for details of preparing appliqués, if necessary. Pin or baste the leaves to the top of the apron in a pleasing arrangement (see figure 15–4 for reference).

2. Draw the vines and tendrils freehand (see figure 15–4).

3M. Machine appliqué the leaves in place as you did on the placemat. Machine embroider the vines as you did on the placemat.

3H. See the general directions for hand appliqué, and appliqué the leaves in place, using hand sewing thread if possible and tiny tacking stitches. Embroider the vines using 3 strands of embroidery floss and the stem stitch. (See the general directions for a diagram of the stem stitch.)

15–4: Apron, showing suggested placement of appliqués and vines.

Full-size leaf patterns. The leaf with tendrils may be used for the napkin corner as well as the placemat and apron.

Desert Nights Lap Quilt and Pillow

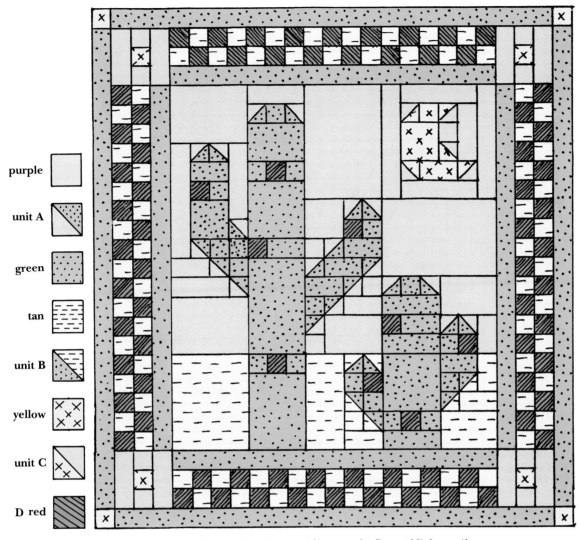

purple

unit A

green

tan

unit B

yellow

unit C

D red

16–1: Construction diagram for Desert Nights quilt.

Materials for the Quilt and Pillow

- 1½ yards deep purple fabric
- 1½ yards green fabric
- 1 yard tan fabric
- ¾ yard red fabric
- ½ yard mustard yellow fabric
- 54 × 58″ piece of fabric for the backing
- 54 × 58″ piece of traditional-weight quilt batting
- All-purpose threads to match the fabrics
- 6 yards of double-fold quilt binding (½″ folded width; 2″ unfolded width); tan in the model)
- 14″ square pillow form
- 14½ × 14½″ piece of batting
- 14½ × 14½″ piece of muslin
- 2 yards of piping for the pillow

The generous size of this lap quilt makes it a perfect snuggler. Deep, rich colors give the feel of a desert night. If you would prefer a desert day, substitute pastels for the dark colors and eliminate the moon area, perhaps appliquéing a bright sun in its place. Finished size of the quilt: 50″ wide × 54″ long. Finished size of the pillow: 14 × 14″.

Directions

All construction is done with right sides of fabric facing and seam allowances of ¼″, which are included in the given measurements. For the quilt, to speed things along, do your cutting first, either with a rotary cutter or scissors. The construction diagram is given in figure 16–1. Figure 16–5 shows the pieces that make up the quilt center. As you cut the pieces, pin those of the same size and color together and tag them with a piece of tape or label so you can find them easily when it comes to construction.

Green fabric cutting guide*

Quantity and Use		Size
FOR THE QUILT		
18	G squares	2½ × 2½"
7	E rectangles	2½ × 4½"
1	F square	4½ × 4½"
2	Q squares	6½ × 6½"
1	N rectangle	4½ × 6½"
1	O rectangle	6½ × 10½"
2	DD rectangles	2½ × 6½"
1	for purple-green two-triangle squares	7 × 16"
1	for tan-green triangle squares	4 × 7"
2	inner border strips	2½ × 34½"
2	inner border strips	2½ × 38½"
2	outer border strips	2½ × 46½"
2	outer border strips	2½ × 50½"
FOR THE PILLOW		
2	strips	2½ × 10½"
2	strips	2½ × 14½"

*Cut the borders first.

Purple fabric cutting guide

Quantity and Use		Size
2	R rectangles	8½" × 12½"
2	H rectangles	6½ × 8½"
2	S rectangles	4½ × 6½"
2	I strips	2½ × 12½"
13	K rectangles*	2½ × 6½"
3	Y rectangles	2½ × 8½"
3	L rectangles	2½ × 4½"
14	U squares*	2½ × 2½"
1	for purple-yellow 2-triangle squares	4 × 7"
1	for purple-green 2-triangle squares	16 × 7"

*2 are for the pillow.

Red fabric cutting guide

Quantity and Use		Size
5	to make borders	2½ × 44"
11	D squares*	2½ × 2½"

*2 are for the pillow.

Yellow fabric cutting guide

Quantity and Use		Size
1	rectangle	4 × 7"
1	BB square	4½ × 4½"
10	AA squares*	2½ × 2½"
1	CC rectangle	2½ × 4½"

*1 is for the pillow.

Tan fabric cutting guide

Quantity and Use		Size
5	for borders	2½" × 44"
1	M rectangle	8½ × 10½"
1	V rectangle	4½ × 10½"
1	for green-tan two-triangle squares	4 × 7"
2	squares*	2½ × 2½"

*For pillow.

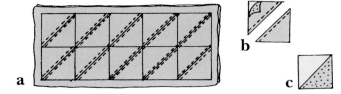

16–2: *Making Unit A (purple-green) two-triangle squares.* **a:** *Marking and sewing.* **b:** *Cutting the units apart on the ruled lines through both layers.* **c:** *The finished Unit A.*

Quilt

1. See the cutting charts for the green, purple, red, and gold fabrics, and cut out and label your fabric pieces.

2. Next, we'll make some two-triangle green-purple A squares by a speed method. On the wrong side of the 16 × 7" green fabric rectangle, mark ten 2⅞" squares. Draw a diagonal line through each square. Take the 16 × 7" purple rectangle and place the two pieces of fabric together, right sides facing. Stitch ¼" from each side of the diagonal lines you drew (figure 16–2a). Cut apart the squares along the marked square lines through both layers of fabric. Then cut each square along the marked diagonal line (figure

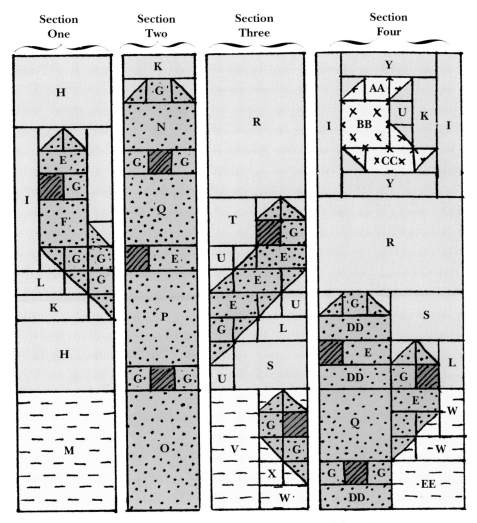

Section One	Section Two	Section Three	Section Four

16–5: Diagram showing the four sections of the quilt center.

16–2b). Press each unit open to make a two-triangle A square as shown (figure 16–2c), for a total of 20 Unit A squares. Set them aside.

3. Take the green 4 × 7″ rectangle and the tan rectangle the same size. Using the same speed method as in Step 2, mark three 2⅞″ squares on the wrong

16–3: Making Unit B (green-tan) two-triangle squares. **a:** *Marking and sewing.* **b:** *The finished unit.*

16–4: Making Unit C (purple-gold) two-triangle squares. **a:** *Marking and sewing.* **b:** *the finished unit.*

side of the tan fabric, mark diagonals, sew the lines, and cut out and press the six two-triangle squares (figure 16–3). Each is a Unit B. Set them aside.

4. Repeat step 3 again, but using the 4 × 7″ rectangle of yellow fabric and one of purple to make six yellow–purple two-triangle squares (Unit C); see figure 16–4. Set them aside.

Piecing the Quilt Center
The quilt center will be pieced in four sections (see figure 16–5). Each section is made up of parts (see figures 16–6, 16–13, 16–14 and 16–20).

SECTION ONE OF THE QUILT CENTER
Look at figure 16–6 to see how the parts are assembled to make Section One. There are two purple H rectangles, a tan M rectangle, and two assembled parts (Part 2 and Part 3). First we'll make the assembled parts.

5. To make Part 2, stitch two of the A units (two-triangle purple-green squares) together with the

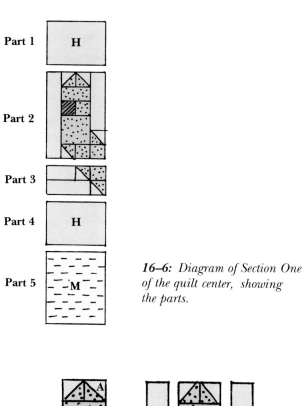

Part 1   H

Part 2

Part 3

Part 4   H

Part 5   M

16–6: Diagram of Section One of the quilt center, showing the parts.

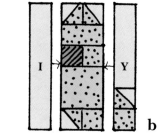

a   **b**

16–7: Part 2 of Section One. **a:** *The center unit.* **b:** *The center-plus side units.*

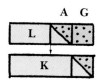

A   G

L

K

16–8: Making Part 3 of Section One.

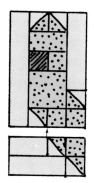

16–9: Joining Part 2 and Part 3 of Section One.

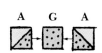

A   G   A

16–10. Making an A-G-A unit for Part 1 of Section Two.

16–11: The finished Part 1 of Section Two.

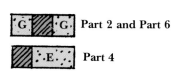

G   G   **Part 2 and Part 6**

E   **Part 4**

16–12: Three more units for Section Two. Top: Part 2 and Part 6. Bottom: Part 4.

green fabric meeting at the center as shown at the top of figure 16–7a. Stitch a 2½ × 4½″ E rectangle just below the joined A units. Stitch a red 2½″ D square to a green 2½″ G square and stitch the D + G squares just below the E strip (see 16–7a). Stitch the green 4½″ F square on next, just below the D + G squares. Press.

6. Stitch the purple 12½″ I strip to the left of the center unit made in step 5, as shown in 16–7b. Set it aside. Stitch an A unit and a green 2½″ G square to the end of the purple 8½″ Y strip and stitch the pieced strip thus formed to the right side of the center unit as shown in 16–7b. Press.

7. To make Part 3, stitch a purple 4½″ L rectangle, an A unit, and a green 2½″ G square together as shown in figure 16–8a (top row). Set it aside. Stitch an A unit to the end of a purple 6½″ K rectangle as shown in 16–8a, bottom. Press. Stitch these two units together as shown in figure 16–8b. This becomes Part 3 for Section One. Join it to Part 2 as shown in 16–9.

8. To assemble Section 1, pin together the units shown in figure 16–6: two H rectangles of purple fabric, a tan M rectangle, and the Part 2 + 3 unit you just completed. Set it aside.

SECTION TWO OF THE QUILT CENTER (SEE FIGURE 16–13)

9. Referring to figure 16–10, stitch together two A units (purple-green two-triangle squares) and a green 2½″ G square. Press.

10. Pin the A-G-A unit made in step 9 between a purple K strip and a green 4½ × 6½″ N rectangle, as shown in figure 16–11, and stitch them together. This is Part 1 of Section Two. Press. Set it aside.

11. Stitch one of the red 2½″ D squares between two green 2½″ G squares (see figure 16–12, top). Make another 3-square unit the same way. Set them aside for Part 2 and Part 6 of Section 2. Stitch one D square to a green E 2½ × 4½″ rectangle (see 16–12, bottom). Press. Set it aside for Part 4 of Section 2.

12. To assemble Section Two, take the green Q, O, and P rectangles and Part 1, 2, 4, and 6 you just made, and pin and stitch them together as shown in figure 16–13. Press. Set Section Two aside.

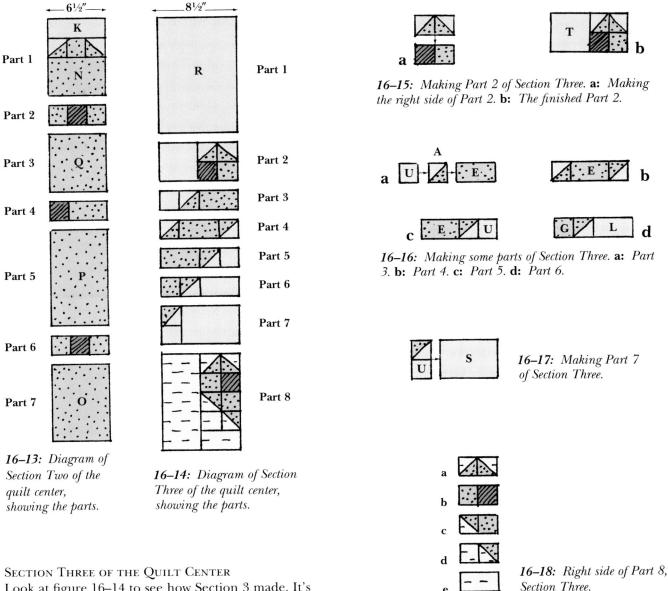

16–13: Diagram of Section Two of the quilt center, showing the parts.

16–14: Diagram of Section Three of the quilt center, showing the parts.

16–15: *Making Part 2 of Section Three.* **a:** *Making the right side of Part 2.* **b:** *The finished Part 2.*

16–16: *Making some parts of Section Three.* **a:** *Part 3.* **b:** *Part 4.* **c:** *Part 5.* **d:** *Part 6.*

16–17: *Making Part 7 of Section Three.*

16–18: *Right side of Part 8, Section Three.*

SECTION THREE OF THE QUILT CENTER

Look at figure 16–14 to see how Section 3 made. It's made up of 8 parts, and 7 of them have to be assembled out of smaller pieces before they are stitched together.

13. First we'll make Part 2. Stitch two A units together with the green sides meeting at the center (figure 16–15a, top). Set it aside. Stitch a 2½″ red D square to a green G square the same size (figure 16–15a, bottom). Referring to 16–15a, join the A-A unit to the D-G unit. Stitch the purple 4½″ T square to the left side of the unit you just made (figure 16–15b). Press. Set it aside as Part 2.

14. Stitch one purple 2½″ U square to an A unit and a green 2½ × 4½″ E rectangle as shown in figure 16–16a. Press. Set it aside as Part 3. Stitch one A unit to each side of a green 2½ × 4½″ E rectangle as shown in figure 16–16b. Press. Set it aside as Part 4. Stitch a green 2½ × 4½″ E strip on one side of an A unit and a purple 2½″ U square to the other side as shown in 16–16c. Press. Set it aside as Part 5. Stitch a green 2½″

G square to one side of an A unit and stitch a 2½ × 4½″ purple L rectangle to the other side as shown in figure 16–16d. Press. Set it aside as Part 6.

15. Stitch an A unit to a 2½″ purple U square (see figure 16–17, left). Stitch this unit to a purple 4½ × 6½″ S rectangle as shown in figure 16–17. Press. Set it aside as Part 7.

16. To make Part 8, look at figure 16–18. We'll work from top to bottom to sew the right half first. Stitch two B units together (figure 16–18a); a B unit is a two-triangle square of green and tan. Set it aside. Stitch a green 2½″ G square to a red D square the same size (figure 16–18b). Set it aside. Stitch one B unit to a green 2½″ G square as shown in figure 16–18c. Set the unit aside. Stitch one tan 2½″ square to a B unit as shown in 16–18d. Lay out the parts from figure 16–18

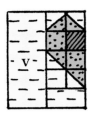

16–19: *The completed Part 8, section Three.*

a through d you just made as shown in the figure and pin them together. Then stitch them together. At the bottom stitch on a tan 2½ × 4½″ W strip (figure 16–18e). This completes the right half of Part 8. Stitch a tan 4½ × 10½″ V rectangle to the left side of Part 8; the complete Part 8 is shown in figure 16–19. Press. Set it aside.

17. Now it's time to assemble Section 3. Lay out all of the parts from 1 through 8, which you made in Steps 13 through 16, along with a purple 8½ × 12½″ R rectangle, as shown in figure 16–14. Pin the pieces together, check the layout, and stitch them together. Press. Set Section 3 aside.

SECTION FOUR OF THE QUILT CENTER
Section Four (see figure 16–20) is made in several parts. First we'll make the top part, the moon block.

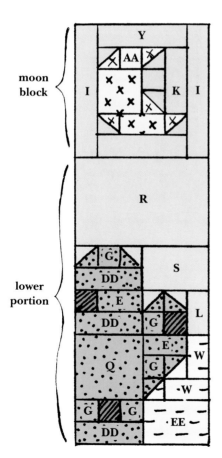

16–20: *Diagram of Section Four of the quilt center, showing the moon block and lower portion. (The moon block plus R = the upper portion.)*

16–21: *Making Part 1 of the center of the moon block. Stitch two C units to a yellow AA square.*

16–22: *Making Part 2 of the center of the moon block.* **a:** *Stitch a U square to a C unit.* **b:** *Stitch a BB square to the U-C unit.*

16–23: *Making Part 3 of the center of the moon block.* **a:** *Stitch a C unit to a CC rectangle.*

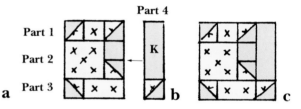

16–24: a: *The joined parts 1 through 3 of the moon block.* **b:** *Adding Part 4 of the center of the moon block.* **c:** *The finished center of the moon block.*

Moon Block
18. To start the moon block, stitch a C unit (a purple-yellow two-triangle square) to each side of a yellow 2½″ AA square as shown in figure 16–21. Press. Set it aside as Part 1 of the moon block.
19. Stitch a C unit to a purple 2½″ U square as shown in figure 16–22a. Stitch the CU unit to the yellow 4½″ BB square as shown in figure 16–22b. Press. Set it aside as Part 2 of the moon block.
20. Stitch one C unit to a yellow 2½ × 4½″ CC rectangle as shown in figure 16–23. Press. It is Part 3 of the moon block.
21. Lay out, pin, and stitch together the Parts 1 through 3 as shown in figure 16–24a. Set it aside. Stitch a C unit to the end of a purple 2½ × 6½″ K rectangle, as shown in figure 16–24b. Press. This is Part 4 of the moon block; stitch it to the right of the unit shown in figure 16–24a. The result (figure 16–24c) is the center of the moon block. Press.
22. Stitch one of the 2½ × 8½″ purple Y strips to the top and one to the bottom edge of the moon block center, as shown in figure 16–25. Press. Stitch a 2½ × 12½″ purple I strip to either side of the moon block (see figure 16–25). Press.

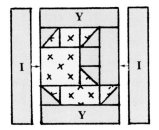

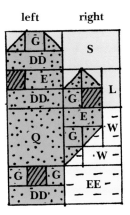

16–25: Attaching the I rectangles to the moon block; the Y rectangles are already attached.

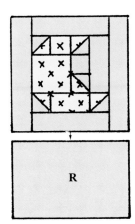

16–26: The upper part of Section Four.

left   right

16–27: The lower unit of Section Four, showing left and right parts.

a   **b**   **c**

*16–28: Making the lower unit of Section Four, left side. **a:** Part 1. **b:** Part 3. **c:** Part 6.*

Part 1
Part 2
Part 3
Part 4

Part 5

Part 6
Part 7

16–29: Diagram of the left part of the lower unit of Section Four, showing parts.

23. Take a purple R rectangle, 12½ × 8½″. Stitch it on a long side just below the moon block (figure 16–26). This completes the upper portion of Section Four. Press it and set it aside.

Lower Unit of Section Four (figure 16–27)
The lower unit of Section Four (see figure 16–5 for reference) is made in two parts: left and right (see figure 16–27). First we'll make the left part.

24. Stitch an A unit to each side of a 2½″ green G square (figure 16–28a). Press. Set it aside as Part 1 of the left side. Stitch one red D square to one green 2½ × 4½″ E strip (figure 16–28b). Set it aside as Part 3 of the left side. Stitch one red D square between two green 2½″ G squares (figure 16–28c). Set it aside as Part 6 of the left side.

25. Lay out, pin and stitch together the 3 assembled units (parts 1, 3 and 6) made in step 24 along with the three green 2½ × 6½″ DD strips and the 6½″ green Q square as shown in figure 16–29. Press. This completes the left side of the lower unit of Section Four.

26. Next we'll make the right part of the lower unit of Section Four. Review it by looking at figure 16–30. Part 1 is simply a purple rectangle, 4½ × 6½″ (S). Set it aside for now. To make Part 2, stitch together two A units, one red D square and one 2½″ green G square

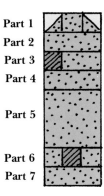

Part 1   **S**

Part 2 {   **G** **L** } **Part 5**

Part 3   **E**
Part 4   **G** **W**

Part 6   ·W·

Part 7   EE

16–30: Diagram of the right part of the lower unit of Section Four, showing parts.

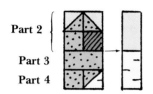

16–31: *Part 2 of the right part of the lower unit of Section Four.*

16–32: *Part 4 of the right part of the lower unit of Section Four.*

Part 2 {
Part 3
Part 4

Part 5

16–33: *Part 5 is sewn to the assembled parts 2, 3, and 4.*

16–34: *W strip is sewn to a B unit to make Part 6 of the right part of the lower unit of Section Four.*

as shown in figure 16–31. Press Part 2 and set it aside.

27. To make Part 4, stitch one of unit B to one green 2½″ G square as shown in figure 16–32. Press it and set it aside.

28. To make Part 5, stitch a tan 2½ × 4½″ W rectangle to a purple L rectangle of the same size, as shown in figure 16–33.

29. Referring to figure 16–33, left, stitch together parts 2, 3, 4, and 5, as shown (Part 3 is a 2½ × 4½″ green rectangle, E).

30. To make Part 6 of the lower right unit, stitch the remaining B unit to the remaining 2½ × 4½″ tan W strip as shown in figure 16–34. Press.

31. Stitch Part 6 to the bottom of the unit made in step 29. Press. Stitch the tan 4½ × 6½″ EE rectangle to the bottom of the unit you just made, as Part 7, referring to figure 16–30. Stitch the purple 4½ × 6½″ S rectangle to the top of the unit. Press. This completes the right part of the lower unit of Section Four.

32. Stitch the right part of the lower unit of Section Four to the left part of the lower unit of section Four, which you completed in Step 25 (see figure 16–35). This completes the lower portion of Section Four.

33. Referring to figure 16–20, stitch the upper portion (completed in step 23) and lower portion of Section Four together to complete it. Press.

34. Referring to figure 16–5, stitch sections One through Four together to make the quilt center. Press.

Corner Units and Borders

Note: See figure 16–40 for all border attachment instructions.

35. To make the corner units for the border, you will need four yellow 2½″ AA squares, eight purple 2½″ U squares, and eight purple 2½ × 6½″ K strips, which

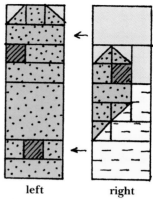

left   right

16–35: *The left and right parts of the lower unit of Section Four are sewn together.*

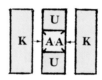

16–36: *A corner unit for the quilt.*

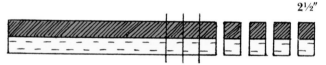

16–37: *Cutting 2-square units for the checkered borders.*

16–38: *A checkered border unit made of 19 red-tan 2-square units.*

you probably already cut. Using one yellow AA square, two purple U squares and two purple K strips, assemble a corner unit as shown in figure 16–36. Press. Make 4 of these corner units and set them aside.

36. Stitch together one red and one tan strip, both 2½ × 44″, along one long edge. Repeat with the remaining 2½ × 44″ red and tan strips to make five 2-strip units. Cut across the joined strips to make 2½″ wide units as shown in figure 16–37. You need 72 of these units for the quilt. Cut 6 extra for the pillow, if you will make the pillow, and set them aside.

37. Making a checkerboard pattern, stitch together 19 of the 2-square red-tan units you just cut together to form a row as shown in figure 16–38. Make another

16–39: A green inner border strip, sewn to a checkered border of 19 units.

16–41: A checkered border unit made of 17 red-tan 2-square units.

19-unit row the same way. Stitch one of the green 2½ × 38½″ inner border strips cut earlier to one side of each of these checkered strips (see figure 16–39) to make a side border unit. Stitch one of these side border units to the left side of the quilt center and one to the right side, with the green strip joining the quilt center (see figure 16–40). Press.

38. Stitch together 17 2-square red-tan units as shown in figure 16–41 to make a border unit for the top of the quilt center. Make another the same way for the bottom of the quilt center. Stitch a green 2½ × 34½″ inner border strip to one side of each of these two border units (figure 16–42).

39. Stitch one of your corner units (made in step 35)

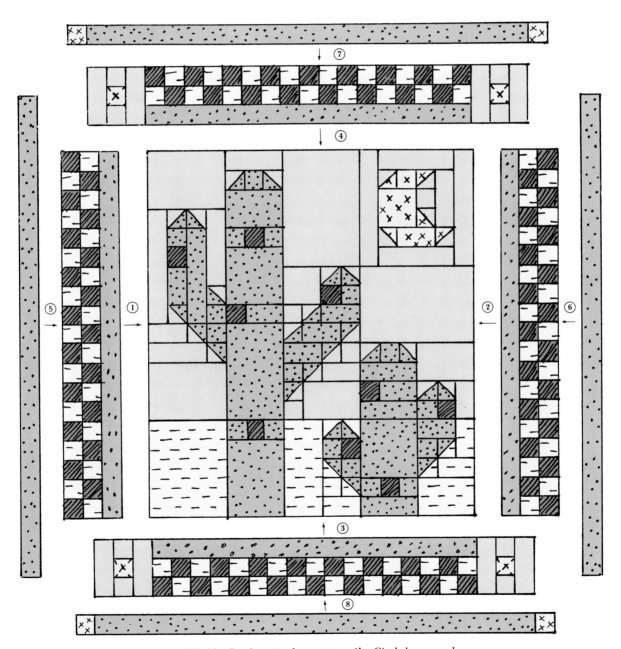

16–40: Border attachment to quilt. Circled numerals indicate order.

16–42: A 17-unit checkered border with corner units and green border strip added.

16–44: Pillow inner borders. **a:** *For top and bottom.* **b:** *For side borders.*

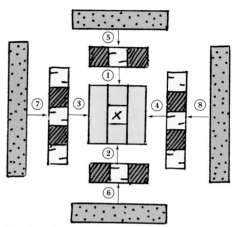

16–43: Pillow construction diagram.

16–45: Attaching pillow borders. Numbers indicate order of piecing.

to each short end of the two border units you made in Step 38 (figure 16–42). Stitch one border unit + corner unit to the top of the quilt center with the green strip edge touching the quilt center (figure 16–40). Stitch the second border unit + corner unit to the bottom of the quilt center. Press.

40. Stitch a green 2½″ × 50½″ outer border strip to the left side of the quilt center. Stitch another one the same size to the right side of the quilt center. Take 4 yellow 2½″ squares, and stitch one to each short end of the two remaining green outer border strips (2½″ × 46″). Stitch one of these border units to the top of the quilt center and one to the bottom of the quilt center (figure 16–40). Press. This completes the quilt top. Hooray!

Basting, Binding, and Quilting

41. Tape the 54 × 58″ backing fabric wrong-side up on your work surface and center the batting over it. Center the quilt top, right side up, over the batting. Hand-baste or pin-baste the layers together. Machine quilt it as desired. (See general instructions for details.)

42. Baste all around the quilt top, about ¼″ in from the raw edge, and trim away the excess batting and

backing that extend beyond the quilt top. Bind the quilt with the bias binding to complete it.

Pillow

1. To make the matching pillow (figure 16–43), make a corner unit as for the quilt (see figure 16–36). Set it aside.

2. Take the 6 extra red-tan 2-square units cut in Step 36 of the quilt project, and two 2½″ red squares and 2 more 2½″ tan squares. Join a 2-square unit to a red square as shown in 16–44a, and attach it to the top of the corner unit (see 16–45). Make another 3-square unit the same way and attach it to the bottom of the corner unit. Make a 5-square unit for the left side of the corner unit and another for the right side (see figure 16–44b). Attach them to the sides of the corner unit as shown in figure 16–45.

3. Take the two green fabric 2½ × 10½″ strips and the two 2½ × 14½″ strips. Attach a 10½″ strip to the top and one to the bottom of the unit you pieced in step 2. Attach the 14½″ green strips to the sides (figure 16–45).

4. Lay out the muslin, with the batting centered over it and the pillow top, face up, centered over the batting and quilt the pillow top as desired. Baste the piping around the edges of the pillow top, with the raw edges facing out.

5. Cut a 14½″ square of any of the leftover fabrics to make the backing for the pillow. Baste the backing to the pillow front, right sides facing, and stitch closed along all 4 sides, leaving a 10″ turning opening along one side. Clip the corners of the seam allowances and turn the pillow covering right-side out. Press. Insert the pillow form and hand-stitch the turning opening closed.

Ocean Breezes Lap Quilt and Pillow Set

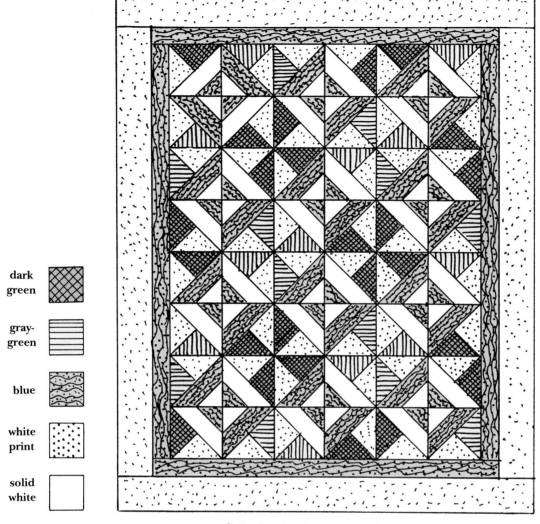

dark
green

gray-
green

blue

white
print

solid
white

17–1: Construction diagram for the quilt.

This quilt may look difficult, but it's a breeze to construct (pardon the pun). Speed cutting (ideal for a rotary cutter) of triangles simplifies the work. Finished size of the quilt: 42 × 52″. There are 12 blocks in the quilt; finished size of one block is 10 × 10″. Finished size of the pillow: 14 × 14″.

Directions

Construction is done with right sides of fabric facing and seam allowances of ¼″, which are included in the given measurements. See fabric cutting guides and cut the pieces you need first.

Quilt
Overview. The construction diagram of the quilt is shown in figure 17–1. The block diagrams are shown

in figure 17–2; there are two kinds of blocks. Each block is made of 4 quarters, which in turn has two halves, a two-triangle half and a half made of two strips. First we'll make the two-strip halves.

1. Take the 7 solid white fabric strips, each 44″ × 2¼″, and the 7 of the same size cut from the dark blue fabric. Stitch one solid white strip to one dark blue strip along one long side. Press. Set it aside. Repeat to make seven 2-strip units.

2. Referring to figure 17–3, from each 2-strip unit cut 45°–90°–45° triangles whose long side is 7¾″, as shown, for a total of fifty-four 2-strip triangles. Half should have dark blue tops; we'll call these s triangles. Half should have solid white tops; we'll call these r triangles. You will need 24 s triangles and 24 r triangles for the quilt; cut two extra of s and 2 of r for the pillow.

Materials for Quilt and Pillow

- 2 yards white print fabric
- 1¼ yards dark blue print or dark blue solid-color fabric
- ¾ yard solid-white fabric
- 23 × 36″ piece of dark green fabric
- 23 × 36″ piece of gray green fabric
- 44 × 54″ piece of traditional-weight quilt batting for the quilt
- 44 × 54″ piece of backing fabric for the quilt
- 15 × 15″ piece of muslin for pillow
- 15 × 15″ piece of batting for pillow
- 15 × 15″ piece of fabric for the pillow backing
- 14″ square pillow form
- 2 yards of piping for the pillow
- Thread to match the fabrics
- 6 yards of double-fold quilt binding (folded width, ½″; unfolded width, 2″); dark green in the model

Dark blue print fabric cutting guide

Quantity and Size		Use
Seven	2¼ × 44″	for triangles
Two	2½ × 34½″*	inner border
Two	2½ × 40½″*	inner border
Two	2½ × 10½″	pillow border
Two	2½ × 14½″	pillow border

Solid white fabric cutting guide

Quantity and Size		Use
Seven	2¼″ × 44″	for triangles

White print fabric cutting guide*

Quantity and Size		Use
Two	4½″ × 44½″*	outer borders
Two	4½″ × 42½″*	outer borders
Two	23 × 36″	for triangles

*Cut the white and dark blue border strips first.

3. Next we'll make the two-triangle corners of the blocks by a speed-triangle method. Take the two white print fabric 23 × 36″ rectangles. On the wrong side of each mark thirteen 6⅜″ squares as shown in figure 17–4a. Mark a diagonal line through each square.

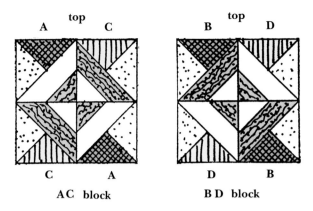

17–2: Block construction diagrams for the quilt, showing the two blocks: the AC block and the BD block.

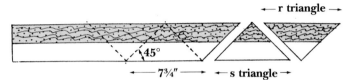

17–3: Cut the 2-strip unit into right triangles as shown; their longest side is 7¾″ units; the small angles are 45°.

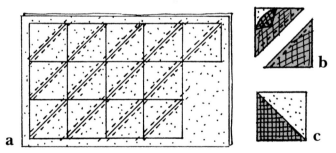

17–4: Making two-triangle squares. **a:** Marking the squares and stitching lines (dashed lines) for two-triangle squares. **b:** Cutting the squares apart. **c:** The pressed two-triangle square.

Take the 23 × 36″ rectangles of the dark green and gray green fabrics also. Place one green rectangle against each marked white print rectangle, right sides together, and stitch ¼″ from each side of the diagonal lines (figure 17–4a). Cut the squares apart along the marked lines and cut along the diagonal markings through both layers of fabric (figure 17–4b). Press each unit open to form a two-triangle square (figure

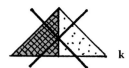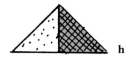

17–5a: *Cut each dark green + white print two-triangle square diagonally into halves; put away or discard the k halves (green on the left) and keep the h halves (green on the right).*

17–5b: *Cut each gray green + white print two-triangle square diagonally into halves; put away or discard the p halves (gray green on the right) and keep the m halves (gray green on left).*

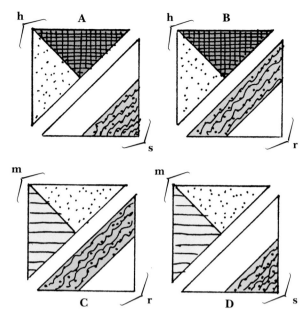

17–6: *Assembly diagrams showing the four kinds of quarters that are used to make blocks. An A quarter = h triangle + s triangle. B quarter = h triangle + r triangle. C quarter = m triangle + r triangle. D quarter = m triangle + s triangle. (Note: this is not a block assembly diagram.)*

17–4c). You will have 52 of these two-triangle squares: 26 dark green + white print and 26 gray green + white print. (This includes enough for the pillow also.)

4. Referring to figure 17–5a, cut each dark green + white print two-triangle square in half diagonally, perpendicular to the line of stitching to make two pieced triangles, for a total of 52 dark green + white print triangles. Look closely at 17–5a. We only want to keep the h dark green + white print triangles, because those are the ones we need in the quilt (and pillow). Carefully take all the others (k triangles) away and put them away for some other project. The h triangles have the dark green side on the right (see 17–5a). You need 24 of them for the quilt (reserve the other 2 for the pillow).

5. Referring to 17–5b, cut each gray green + white print square in half diagonally, perpendicular to the line of stitching, to make two pieced triangles, for a total of 56 gray green + white print triangles. Look closely at 17–5b. We only want to keep the m gray green + white print triangles; those are the ones we need in the quilt. The m triangles are the ones with light green on the left side. You need 24 of them for the quilt and two for the pillow. Carefully take all the others (p triangles) away and put them away for some other project.

6. Now we can start assembling the 4 quarters that make up each block in the quilt. There are four different kinds of quarters, A, B, C, and D (see figure 17–6). For the quilt blocks we need to make:

    14 A quarters   14 C quarters
    10 B quarters   10 D quarters

7. To make quarter A, stitch an h triangle (from step 4) to an s triangle from step 2, as shown in figure 17–6. Repeat to make a total of 14 A quarters. Set them aside.

8. To make quarter B, stitch an h triangle to an r triangle (from step 2). Repeat to make a total of 10 B quarters. Set them aside.

9. To make quarter C, stitch an m triangle (from step 5) to an r triangle. Repeat to make a total of 14 C quarters. Set them aside.

10. To make quarter D, stitch an m triangle to an s triangle. Repeat to make a total of 10 D quarters. Now we can assemble our blocks from the quarters.

11. *The AC blocks:* Look at the AC block in figure 17–2. Take 2 A quarters and 2 C quarters, position them as shown in 17–2 to make an AC block, pin them together, and stitch them together. Make a total of 7 AC blocks the same way. Press them and set them aside.

12. *The BD blocks:* Look at the BD block in figure 17–2. We need to make 5 BD blocks for the quilt. For the pillow, make one more. Take two B quarters and 2 D quarters, position them as shown in 17–2 to make a BD block, pin them together, and stitch them together. Make a total of 5 BD blocks the same way. Press them and set them aside.

13. Now we're ready to assemble the blocks into the quilt center. We need to make 4 rows of three blocks

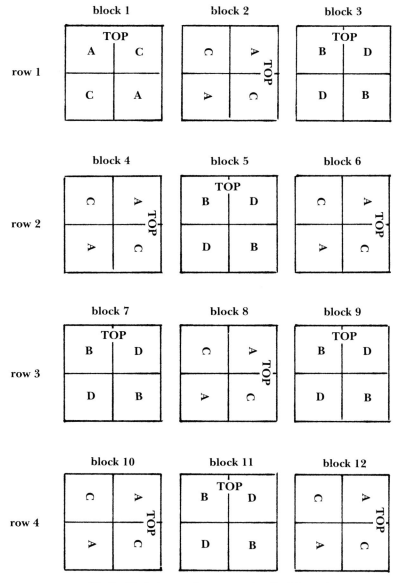

17–7: *Block layout for center of quilt. Note orientation of tops of blocks.*

each. See figure 17–7 for guidance in positioning the blocks. Be sure to note how the top of the block is turned in the row. Pin the blocks together for row 1, check it with the construction diagram (figure 17–1), and stitch the blocks together. Tag the row with masking tape and set the row aside. Repeat the same procedure for rows 2 through 4.

14. Once the blocks are sewn into rows, pin the rows together, check their positioning with figure 17–1, and stitch row 1 to row 2, etc., until you have completed the quilt center.

15. Take 2 dark blue 34½″ inner border strips. Stitch one to the left and one to the right of the quilt center; see figure 17–1 for reference. Press. Take two

40″ dark blue border strips. Stitch one strip to the top and one to the bottom of the quilt center.

16. Take two white print 42½″ outer border strips. Stitch one to the left and one to the right of the unit you made in step 15. Take two white print 44½″ border strips. Stitch one print border strip to the top and one to the bottom of the unit. Press. This completes your quilt top.

17. *Basting, Quilting, and Binding.* Tape the quilt backing to your work surface, wrong side up, and center the batting over it. Center the quilt top right-side up over the batting. Hand-baste or pin-baste the layers together. Quilt as desired (see general instructions).

18. After quilting, baste all around the quilt top, about ¼″ in from the raw edges of the quilt top, and trim away any excess batting and backing fabric that extend beyond the quilt top. Bind the quilt to complete it (see general instructions).

Pillow

1. For the pillow, make one block as you did for the quilt.
2. Take the two dark blue fabric 2½ × 10½″ strips and two 2½ × 14½″ strips. Stitch the 10½″ long strips to two opposite sides of the block, referring to figure 17–8. Then stitch the 14½″ strips to the remaining two sides.
3. Tape the muslin square to your work surface, center the batting square over it, and the pillow top face up over that. Quilt the pillow as desired.
4. Baste about ¼″ in from the raw edges of the pillow top all around, and trim away the excess batting and backing that extends beyond the pillow top. Baste the piping around the edges of the pillow top, with raw edges out, and stitch the backing to the pillow top, with its right side facing the right side of the pillow

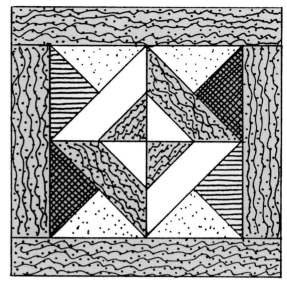

17–8: The pillow top.

top, along all 4 sides, leaving a 10″ opening for turning. Clip the corners of the seam allowance and turn the pillow covering right-side out. Insert the pillow form and hand-stitch the turning opening closed to complete the pillow.

Patriotic Pillows and Placemat Set

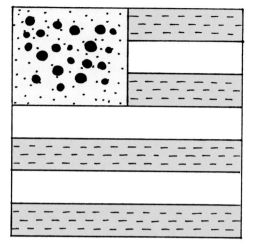

18–1: *Construction diagram of the flag pillow. Dark circles indicate suggested button placement.*

blue

off-white

red

These pieced pillows and placemat are quick and easy to stitch. The deep colors and buttons in varying sizes give the projects a "country" character. For a time-worn look, try using light red and blue fabrics with tea-dyed muslin for the off-white fabric. Finished size of each pillow: 14 × 14″. Finished size of placemat: 18 × 14″.

Materials Needed for All Projects

- ½ yard red fabric
- ½ yard blue fabric
- ½ yard off-white fabric
- 1 yard fabric for backings
- 1 yard low-loft batting
- 3½ yards of piping for the pillows
- Two 14″ pillow forms
- Two 16½″ squares of muslin
- 35 to 48 assorted buttons
- All-purpose thread to match fabrics

Directions

All construction is done with right sides of fabric facing and seam allowances of ¼″, which are included in the measurements given. After piecing, press seam allowances towards the darker color. Referring to the cutting guides, cut all the pieces you need for all three projects.

Flag Pillow (figure 18–1)

1. Stitch a 2½″ × 40″ off-white strip between two red strips of the same size to make a 3-strip unit, as shown

Red fabric cutting guide

Quantity and Size		Use
Two	2½ × 40″	flag pillow
Two	2½ × 14½″	placemat
One	4½ × 4½″	patchwork pillow
One	2½ × 30″	patchwork pillow
Two	2½ × 10½″	placemat

Blue fabric cutting guide

Quantity and Size		Use
One	6½ × 7½″	flag pillow
Four	6½ × 6½″	pieced pillow
Four	2½ × 6½″	placemat
Two	2½ × 14½″	placemat

Off-white fabric cutting guide

Quantity and Size		Use
One	2½ × 40″	flag pillow
Two	2½ × 30″	pieced pillow
Four	2½ × 2½″	placemat
One	2½ × 14½″	flag pillow

Batting cutting guide

Quantity and Size		Use
Two	16½ × 16½″	flag and pieced pillow
One	14½ × 16½″	placemat

Backing fabric cutting guide

Quantity and Size		Use
Two	14½ × 14½″	flag and pieced pillow
One	14½ × 18½″	placemat

in figure 18–2. Press the seam allowances towards the red fabric. Cut off two pieces from the 3-strip unit: one 7½″ length and one 14½″ length (see figure 18–2).

2. Stitch a 2½ × 14½″ off-white strip to one long edge of the 14½″ 3-strip unit (see figure 18–3). Press. This completes the lower section.

3. Stitch the blue 6½ × 7½″ piece to a 6½″ side of the 7½″ long 3-strip piece made in step 1. This completes the upper flag section (figure 18–4). Press.

4. Stitch the upper and lower sections together as shown in figure 18–5 to complete the pillow top. Press.

5. Center a 16½″ square of batting over a muslin square of the same size. Center the pieced pillow top over the batting. Pin-baste or hand baste the layers

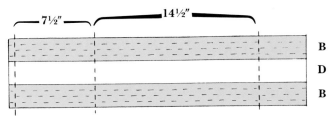

18–2: Cutting 3-strip pieces for the flag pillow.

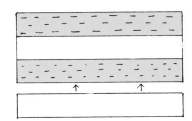

18–3: Stitching a strip to the 14½"-wide 3-strip piece for the flag pillow.

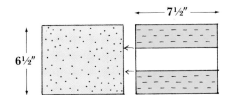

18–4: Stitching a blue square to a 7½"-wide 3-strip piece for the flag pillow.

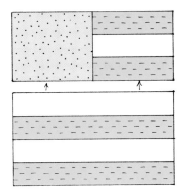

18–5: Stitching the upper flag section to the lower section.

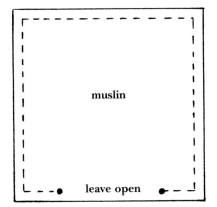

18–6: Stitch around the pillow top, leaving a turning opening at the bottom.

together and hand quilt or machine quilt as desired. Trim off any excess batting or muslin that extends beyond the pillow top.

6. Baste the piping around the edges of the pillow top with its raw edge facing out, aligned with the raw edges of the pillow top. (See general directions on piping.)

7. Stitch the pillow top to a 14½" square of backing fabric with right sides facing, around all 4 sides, leaving a 12" opening along the bottom edge for turning (figure 18–6). Clip the corners of the seam allowances and turn the pillow cover right-side out. Insert the pillow form and hand-stitch the opening closed.

8. Stitch the buttons to the blue area of the pillow top, referring to figure 18–1 (black dots show suggested button placement).

Pieced pillow (figure 18–7)

1. Stitch a 2½ × 30" red strip between 2 off-white strips the same size, as shown in figure 18–8, to make

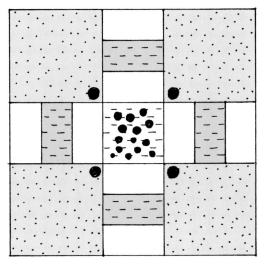

18–7: Construction diagram for the pieced pillow. Black circles indicate suggested button placement.

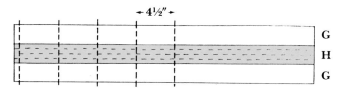

18–8: Cutting unit A for the pieced pillow.

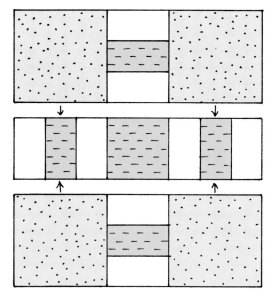

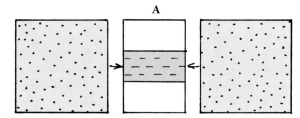

18–9: Stitching 2 squares to unit A to form a row for the pieced pillow.

18–11: Stitching the 3 rows together to make the pillow top (pieced pillow).

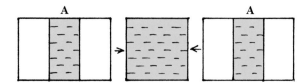

18–10: Stitching two of unit A to a red square to form a row.

a 3-strip unit. Press. Cut off four 4½″-wide A units across all 3 strips (see 18–8). Save the remainder of the 3-strip unit for the placemat.

2. Stitch a 6½″ blue square to each long side of an A unit (see figure 18–9) to make a row. Repeat to make another row just like it. Press. Set them aside.

3. Stitch two A units to the 4½″ red square as shown in figure 18–10. Press.

4. Stitch the two rows made in step 2 to the row made in step 3, as shown in figure 18–11. Press.

5. Follow steps 5 through 7 of the flag pillow instructions to finish the pieced pillow. Attach the buttons, referring to figure 18–7.

Placemat (figure 18–12)

1. To make the placemat, take the leftover 3-strip (off-white—red—off-white) from step 1 of the pieced pillow and cut across all strips to make three 2½″-wide B units, as shown in figure 18–13.

2. Stitch the 3 B units, alternating with four 2½ × 6½″ blue pieces, as shown in figure 18–14, to make the placemat center. Press.

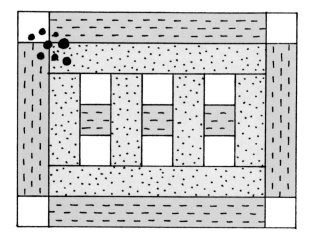

18–12: Construction diagram of the placemat top.

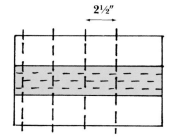

18–13: Cutting B units for the placemat top.

3. Stitch two 2½″ × 14½″ blue strips to the placemat center as shown in figure 18–15. Press.

4. Refer to figure 18–16 while doing the following.

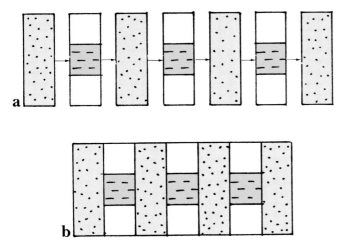

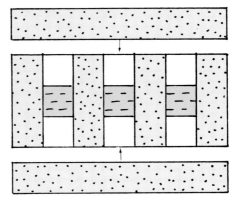

18–15: Adding blue strips to the placemat center.

a

b

18–14: Assembling the placemat center.

Stitch two 2½ × 14½″ red strips to the placemat
center. Stitch one off-white 2½″ square to each short
end of a 2½ × 10½″ red strip to make a border strip.
Stitch each border strip to the sides of the placemat as
shown to complete the placemat top. Press.

5. Take the 14½ × 18½″ piece of batting and baste it
to the back side of the pieced placemat top. Pin the
placemat top to the 14½ × 18½″ piece of backing
fabric, with right sides facing, and stitch them
together along all 4 sides, leaving a 6″ turning
opening along one long edge. Clip the corners of the
seam allowances and turn the placemat right-side out.
Hand-stitch the turning opening closed. Pin-baste or
baste the layers of the placemat together and hand-
quilt or machine-quilt the placemat as you wish.

6. Stitch the buttons to one corner of the placemat as
shown in figure 18–12 to complete it. Black dots
indicate suggested button placement.

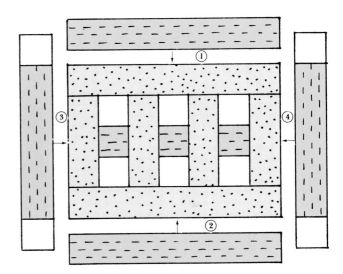

18–16: Adding borders to the placemat center.

Quilting Patterns

Small border buds.

Small flower pattern.

Medium-sized border repeat.

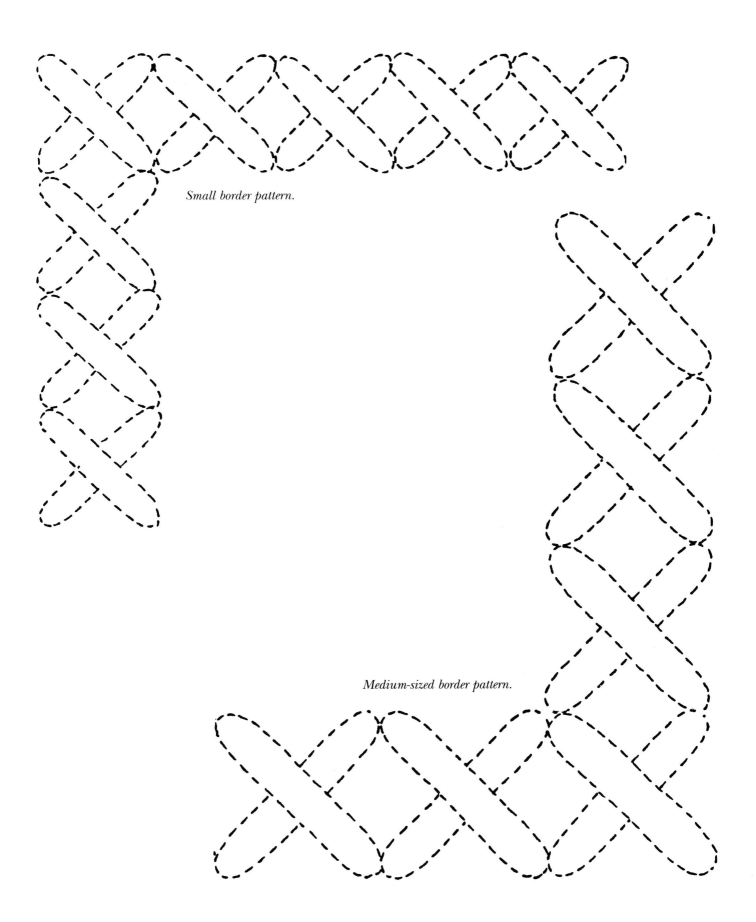

Small border pattern.

Medium-sized border pattern.

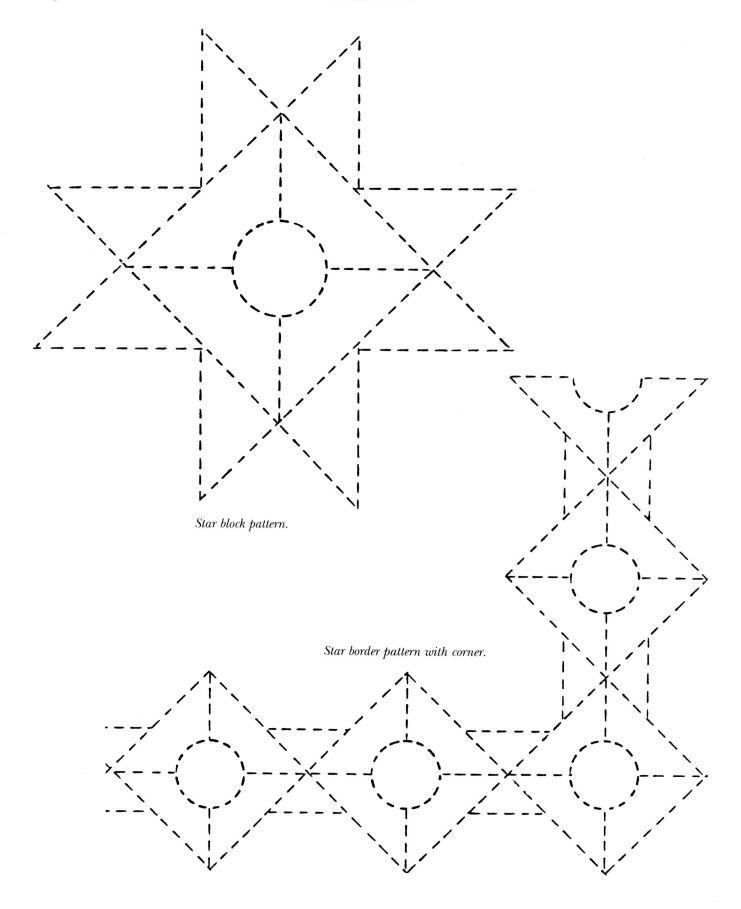

Star block pattern.

Star border pattern with corner.

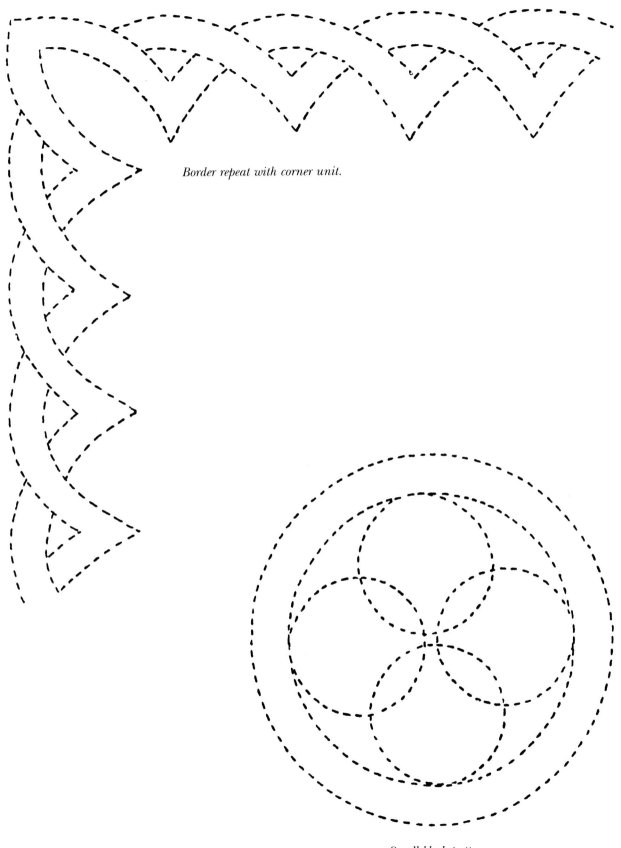

Border repeat with corner unit.

Small block pattern.

Small block pattern.

Small border pattern with corner.

Index

Useful Tables

A. Metric Equivalents:
Inches to Millimetres (mm) and Centimetres (cm)

Inches	mm	cm	Inches	cm	Inches	cm
⅛	3	0.3	9	22.9	30	76.2
¼	6	0.6	10	25.4	31	78.7
⅜	10	1.0	11	27.9	32	81.3
½	13	1.3	12	30.5	33	83.8
⅝	16	1.6	13	33.0	34	86.4
¾	19	1.9	14	35.6	35	88.9
⅞	22	2.2	15	38.1	36	91.4
1	25	2.5	16	40.6	37	94.0
1¼	32	3.2	17	43.2	38	96.5
1½	38	3.8	18	45.7	39	99.1
1¾	44	4.4	19	48.3	40	101.6
2	51	5.1	20	50.8	41	104.1
2½	64	6.4	21	53.3	42	106.7
3	76	7.6	22	55.9	43	109.2
3½	89	8.9	23	58.4	44	111.8
4	102	10.2	24	61.0	45	114.3
4½	114	11.4	25	63.5	46	116.8
5	127	12.7	26	66.0	47	119.4
6	152	15.2	27	68.6	48	121.9
7	178	17.8	28	71.1	49	124.5
8	203	20.3	29	73.7	50	127.0

B. Yards Into Inches

Yards	Inches	Yards	Inches
⅛	4.5	1⅛	40.5
¼	9	1¼	45
⅜	13.5	1⅜	49.5
½	18	1½	54
⅝	22.5	1⅝	58.5
¾	27	1¾	63
⅞	31.5	1⅞	67.5
1	36	2	72